"It's been a long time since I've seen such an authentic book that tells the story of food. It's not overdone, not too complicated and not pretentious. At the end of the day, chefs and food lovers are all looking for ideas and inspiration. This book gives us exactly that. Well done!"

—**RAN SHMUELI**, Israeli celebrity chef and judge on *Iron Chef Israel*

"Each recipe in this book is carefully crafted with a story to tell. This is a must-have on any bookshelf."

—**TODD SUGIMOTO**, executive chef at La Pizza La Pasta and Eataly Las Vegas

"Danielle has a way of elevating everyday recipes to make them fabulous and delicious in a easy and approachable way. She really teaches the cook how to understand the food and the flavors to create something very special."

—**JOSH CAPON**, executive chef and partner at Lure Fishbar

"Danielle's recipes are always exciting to make—she adds a unique Middle Eastern twist to familiar dishes, taking them to a whole new level."

—**FELICITY SPECTOR**, journalist and Great Taste Award judge

FOOD YOU LOVE
BUT DIFFERENT.

**EASY AND EXCITING WAYS
TO ELEVATE YOUR FAVORITE MEALS**

DANIELLE ORON

author of *Modern Israeli Cooking*

PAGE STREET
PUBLISHING CO.

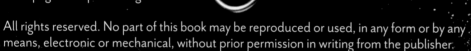

THIS BOOK IS FOR ZOE.

CONTENTS

MORNINGS 17

PASTA 38

TURF & SURF 65

CHICKEN & POTATOES 66
Instant Pot Shredded Chicken/Mashed Potatoes/
Cumin Tzatziki

STEAK 71
Shabu-Shabu Cut/Chile-Lime Butter

MEATBALLS 72
Harissa/Mozzarella/Sandwich Optional

CHEESEBURGER 74
Cumin/Über-Thin Ground Chuck/Basic White Bread

SALMON 79
Harissa/Soy/Castelvetrano Olives

MEAT LOAF 80
Baharat/Dried Cherries/Olives/Silan Soy Glaze

PAILLARD 83
Turmeric/Cumin/Radish & Cabbage Sumac Slaw

SHRIMP & GRITS 84
Curry/Cream Cheese Grits

PULLED PORK 87
Kimchi/Gochujang/Sorghum/Soy Sauce

PORK CHOPS 88
Urfa Pico de Gallo/Tahini

CHICKEN SOUP 91
Hominy/Poblano/Cheez-Its

FISH & CHIPS 92
Hawaij/Salt & Vinegar Chips

SHAWARMA 95
Harissa Mayo/Pickles

VEGETABLES & RICE 96

FRIED RICE 98
Curry/Coconut Milk

MASHED POTATOES 101
White Sweet Potatoes/Brown Butter/Vanilla Bean/
Almonds

BROCCOLINI 102
Shawarma Spice/Tahini Sauce/Lemon

PANZANELLA 105
Za'atar/Olives/Mozzarella/Sumac Sourdough

GREEN BEANS 106
Snow Peas/Za'atar/Yogurt

SLAW 109
Sumac/Pepitas/Sunflower Seeds/Blue Cheese

CAESAR 110
Tahini/Avocado/Sumac Croutons

CELERY 113
White Pepper/Goat Cheese/Hazelnuts

WHITE RICE 114
Cucumbers/Cashews/Cilantro/Mint

RICE & BEANS 117
Baharat/Black Beans/Olives/Bananas

INTRODUCTION

I was once a restaurant chef and a bakery owner. I strongly believed you had to make your own aioli and three-tiered birthday cakes. Having the time and luxury on my hands to focus solely on how to create interesting dishes was something I really enjoyed. But now I am a mother who works from home, and the days seem to get shorter and shorter. As my family grew and our daughter, Zoe, was born, I quickly realized that I had to simplify my (food) life to match our lifestyle. My family believes that it's more important to spend time together than to spend hours in the kitchen cooking, so I've changed my approach. I now classify myself not as a chef, but as a home cook. And I'm pretty damn proud of it.

But there is still the constant battle with dinner. What's for dinner? Ugh, but chicken again? These are the conversations I have with myself and my husband when trying to figure out what to make. It's a never-ending story. We always end up eating the same things. But guess what? *That's okay.* My daughter has taught me a very important lesson: Not every meal needs to be a production. You do not need to reinvent the wheel every time. Leaning back is acceptable. *You're making food to feed yourself, and that is what is important.*

To fight dinner boredom without spending hours in the kitchen, I learned to stick with the meals I know, but tweak them to make them taste new and exciting. Think of that thing you always resort to making. K, got it in your head? Now, what can you add in or swap out to change it? Can you add a spice? Try turmeric or curry. Slice that vegetable differently and give it a moment. Using rice? Try freekeh. How about you grill that string bean? Okay, now just cover it with za'atar. Put ranch dressing on it! No, never mind, don't do that. Catch my flow yet? Making chicken (again)? Cut it thinly, pound it out. Add acid; olives are amazing. Tear that olive apart! Chimichurri. Always, chimichurri.

For me—and now you, because you have this book in your hands—it looks like my mom's basic Bolognese but with chorizo and red wine. My morning fried egg but with curry powder. Baharat-spiced meat loaf with cherries and pistachios. Familiar dishes, but with a twist that elevates them. That's how this cookbook was born.

My publisher and I brainstormed titles for this book and came up with a few that we felt didn't really stick: *Untraditional. Keep It Simple, Stupid. Not Your Mama's Cookbook. On the Usual.* It's hard picking a title. Then, my dad came over and hopped on my computer to play around with a cover idea. I walked away and when I came back I saw "Food You Love but a Bit Different." As I sat there looking at it, I started to realize how perfectly genius my dad is. It's exactly what this collection of recipes is. Those things I grew up loving but have become so tired of that I've changed them in a way to make them fresh and new.

So, there you have it. These recipes will allow you to keep meals interesting without spending forever in the kitchen cooking. They're easy and accessible and will make a familiar meal exciting again. This book is for any busy family trying to get something on the table, for a novice home cook trying something new and for anyone who is bored with the same old stuff he or she has been cooking up at home.

It's very easy to take something you already know and to spruce it up. Don't be afraid to add some spunk. Toss in a twist. Give it a new life. It's the food you love, but different.

NOTES FOR THE BRAIN AND THE TASTE BUDS

NOTES ON SALT

There are two questions that I dread when teaching or writing: "How much salt?" and "What's the best kind of salt to use?" First, how much salt will depend on what kind of salt you're using and your palate. The answer to the second would be to use the kind of salt you're already using. I don't care whether it's fancy, expensive salt or Morton's salt. The salt you are currently using is what you're used to seasoning your food with. Stick to it. You know it. But if you must know, I use Diamond Crystal kosher salt for seasoning and cooking and Maldon sea salt for finishing. That is what my hand and palate are used to.

Little story about salt: While I was consulting at a restaurant, our delivery guy switched the brand of kosher salt from Diamond Crystal to Morton's. Our cooks did everything per usual, but *everything* was twice as salty that day. We all had to adjust our hand and it took a bit of getting used to. Don't mess with the salt.

Basic rules of thumb for salt: Use kosher salt to season as you're cooking. Use a flaky sea salt to garnish and finish dishes. Table salt is exactly that . . . for the table, preferably in a cute, vintage shaker.

A pinch of salt: When you read "pinch of salt" in any of these recipes, I want you to stick all five of your fingers into the salt container and grab a nice, healthy pinch. Don't be shy.

NOTES ON BLACK PEPPER

Please get yourself a pepper grinder. The only time you can use already ground black pepper is if you're at the diner and you order egg salad. It's just not great, cooks.

Black pepper knowledge: The more you use, the more you need the next time. It's known to be addictive, like drugs. I'm not a doctor, though.

How to use black pepper: Lightly toast your black peppercorns in a dry pan over medium-low heat until just slightly fragrant, let them cool, then fill your pepper grinder.

NOTES ON SEASONING

Seasoning as you go: You want to be sure that you're adding a little bit of salt as you cook. This develops a different flavor than if you were to just season at the end. Just be sure you aren't oversalting. When you season as you go, you should be gentle.

Seasoning from above: Be super-generous. Grab lots of salt and season from high above; that way, it rains down *evenly* on the meat, chicken, fish, vegetables or whatever else you're seasoning before searing or roasting. Use the pepper grinder from up high as well.

NOTES ON TASTING

Taste as you go. Heard? Ingredient brands are different. Fruits, vegetables, beef, chicken, pork, seafood and so on all taste different depending on their freshness and where they come from. The most important thing you can do when you cook is to taste. Forget about the recipe. If you taste the food as you cook, you will know whether you need more acid or more sweetness by trusting your own taste buds. It doesn't matter what it's "supposed to taste like," it should just taste good to you when you're cooking.

NOTES ON *MISE EN PLACE*

When you're following a recipe, make sure all your ingredients are ready to go. If the recipe calls for diced onions, sliced peppers and grated garlic, make sure you have those diced, sliced, grated and ready to go before you turn on the heat under your pan. Pull out all the spices you need. This way you're prepared and set to cook. You can give your full attention to what is happening in the pan as opposed to running around the kitchen looking for that paprika while your garlic burns.

NOTES ON MAKING A MESS

When your creative juices are flowing, make an honest disaster. Don't stress about the mess in the moment. Turn the whole kitchen upside down. Use every pan, dish and gadget you've got.

NOTES ON *NOT* FOLLOWING A RECIPE

Trust your instincts. Recipes are more like guidelines than strict law. Cook with feeling. Read the recipe through to understand the ingredients and the technique, but then go ahead and cook with your feelings. Feel the food. Don't let following the recipe blind you. Be present and feel. *So poetic.*

NOTES ON FOLLOWING A RECIPE

If you're *baking*, follow the recipe.

MORNINGS

I LOVE MY HUSBAND, BUT HE CAN'T COOK. He does two things well: He can boil a perfect six-minute egg (page 129) and makes a damn good bowl of cereal. He's also our coffee guy in the morning, brewing an excellent French press. On every occasion, I'm the food person in the family. I still love you, Tas.

No matter how much my stomach turns at cooking first thing in the morning, I basically *have* to, or else my daughter and husband will starve before 9:30 a.m. Morning meals need to be simple, filling, but most important, exciting, because I just do not have it in me to make boring eggs anymore.

We used to have the luxury of hanging around the house until 10 and then running out to get bagels or a nice brunch. I used to have the pleasure of leisurely opening the fridge and taking my time making *shakshuka* on a Saturday. But this tiny girl came into our lives and changed everything. So now, it's *wake-up-what's-breakfast*. She goes from super-cute morning face to hangry in the blink of an eye. I hope this changes as she gets older. This means that Mom needs to wake up and make something before she's opened her eyes. Boy, is that fun.

I just can't spend too much time making breakfast and brunch anymore. So, these are some of my upgraded and updated recipes for when it comes to morning eats. These are all recipes that can be made for 1 or for 10 very easily with flavors that will wake you up and fill your belly. I honestly believe that all these morning meals are exciting enough to serve to a group of friends for brunch and also as a simple breakfast for your family. Our favorites include the crepes (page 29), which can be made ahead of time, and the tacos (page 33) because they literally take no time.

BREAKFAST SANDWICH

URFA BIBER/KALE/RICOTTA

Makes 4 sandwiches

The breakfast sandwich is a very personal thing. I like mine on a bagel with egg and Swiss, tomato, mayo, salt and pepper. In New York City, the classic is bacon, egg and American cheese on a kaiser roll. At McDonald's, the Sausage McMuffin rules. It's whatever is comforting and good in the moment.

This is the sandwich I make to get my greens in. It works with any type of kale, collards or chard. The greens are sautéed quickly in olive oil and Urfa biber, a chile flake that's smoky and almost sweet. I love ricotta in a sandwich, as it's super-creamy and light. The yolk is the beautiful sauce that drapes over the deep green of the kale and the stark white ricotta. Poetry. I would happily eat the sautéed kale over hummus with a fried egg. You can also try some sriracha on top for added heat.

THE THINGS

1 tbsp (15 ml) olive oil

1 to 2 cloves garlic, grated on a microplane

1 tsp Urfa biber

2 cups (134 g) stemmed and roughly chopped curly kale

1 tsp fresh lemon juice

Kosher salt

1 cup (250 g) smooth ricotta cheese

4 English muffins, toasted

4 fried eggs (page 30, minus the curry powder)

Flaky sea salt

Freshly ground black pepper

THE WAY

In a large skillet, heat the olive oil over medium-low heat. Add the garlic and Urfa and cook until fragrant, about 30 seconds. Add the kale and cook, tossing occasionally, until wilted, 1½ to 2 minutes. Season with the lemon juice and kosher salt.

Spread ¼ cup (62 g) of the ricotta on the bottom half of each English muffin. Top with the sautéed kale and a fried egg and season to taste with flaky salt and black pepper.

SCRAMBLED EGGS

TURMERIC/RED ONION/
CHERRY TOMATOES/YOGURT

Makes 4 servings

I really hope you make scrambled eggs at home. Once you've mastered your own technique, it becomes second nature, but, hell, it can be blah. We've become increasingly bored with a plain butter scramble in my family since making it so often. So, we began to tweak it: extra butter and cheese, super-herby, curry powder (it's delicious), salami, za'atar and so on. After going to one of our favorite Persian spots for brunch in Toronto, I was inspired to cook this up one morning.

This recipe is quick, flavorful, tangy, creamy and spicy, and the color is beautiful. A quick sauté in butter and oil softens the onion, gets some of that juice out of the tomatoes and brings out the flavor and aroma of the turmeric. Then, you just add the eggs and a minute or two later, it's done. A dollop of labne or Greek yogurt is perfect on top for a cooling factor to the turmeric. Chives are cute. I've put these eggs in a pita with avocado for an on-the-go breakfast.

THE THINGS

6 large eggs

Kosher salt

Freshly ground black pepper

1 tbsp (15 ml) olive oil

2 tbsp (28 g) unsalted butter

½ red onion, sliced very thinly

8 to 12 cherry tomatoes, halved

1¼ tsp (3 g) ground turmeric

Dollops of labne or Greek yogurt, for serving

Chopped fresh chives, for serving

Toasted crusty bread, for serving

THE WAY

Whisk the eggs in a bowl and season with a bit of salt and pepper.

In a large, nonstick skillet, heat the oil and butter over medium heat. Add the onion and tomatoes and cook until softened, 3 to 4 minutes. Add the turmeric and cook until fragrant, about another minute. Pour the eggs into the pan and cook, stirring with a heatproof rubber spatula, until the eggs are set, about 2 minutes. Season again with salt and pepper.

Divide the eggs among 4 plates and dollop each serving with labne. Garnish with chives and serve with toasted bread.

SMOOTHIE BOWL

SKYR/TAHINI/BANANA

Makes 2 bowls

I'm somewhat of a yogurt snob. I like thick and creamy yogurt, always as a late-night treat, never in the morning. I cover it with tahini and sprinkle so many chocolate sprinkles on top that the yogurt totally gets lost (this is where you can judge me). I switched from full-fat Greek yogurt to a low-fat Icelandic skyr when my jeans started tightening from my midnight snacks. It could also be those cookie dough balls from the freezer that I eat like popcorn. I need to check myself.

If you haven't had Icelandic skyr yet, you have not lived. Super-thick, it's hefty but spoonable and reminds me of something you'd find between Greek yogurt and labne. It's on the upward trend and can be found at almost all grocery stores. My favorite is either plain or vanilla, but Icelandic Provisions makes a coconut one that's making its way up my ranks.

THE THINGS

2 cups (460 g) skyr or Greek yogurt

1 banana

½ cup (120 g) tahini

½ cup (120 ml) milk

2 tbsp (40 g) honey or silan (date syrup)

1 tsp vanilla bean paste

To Serve

Banana slices

Pistachios

Bran or other whole-grain cereal or granola

Honey or silan

Black sesame seeds

THE WAY

In a blender, combine the skyr, banana, tahini, milk, honey and vanilla bean paste and blend until smooth.

To serve, pour into 2 bowls and top with banana slices, pistachios, bran, honey and sesame seeds.

OATMEAL

CHEDDAR/KIMCHI/EGG

Makes 4 servings

I made a version of this oatmeal on my blog. It was one of my more genius moments—*brushes shoulder off*. It was a "bacon" and eggs oatmeal made with crispy sorghum and smoked sea salt chicken skin and a poached egg over savory oatmeal. Re-grammed, tweeted, blogged about like crazy, and I thought it was the best thing in the world. It totally is.

This is a version of that but simpler and with Korean flavor. The oatmeal plays like cheesy grits in a way, making it the base of a simple and easy breakfast bowl. Try using Parmesan instead of sharp cheddar for a cacio e pepe oatmeal! Make a six-minute egg or fry one up, but if you have some extra time, sous vide the shit out of that egg. If you are in a pinch, use quick-cooking oats. Just cook them as directed on the package and add the cheese.

THE THINGS

3½ cups (828 ml) water

½ cup (120 ml) whole milk

1 cup (80 g) steel-cut oats

Kosher salt

1 cup (115 g) shredded sharp white cheddar cheese

Freshly ground black pepper

To Serve

1 cup (150 g) chopped cabbage kimchi

4 six-minute large eggs (page 129) or fried eggs (page 30, minus the curry powder)

Black sesame seeds

Flaky sea salt

THE WAY

In a saucepan with a tight-fitting lid, bring the water and milk to a boil over medium-high heat. Stir in the oats and a healthy pinch of kosher salt. Lower the heat to low, cover and simmer, stirring occasionally, until the oats are cooked through and creamy, about 30 minutes. Mix in the cheddar and season with additional salt and pepper.

To serve, divide the oatmeal among 4 bowls and top each with chopped kimchi and a cooked egg. Garnish with black sesame seeds and flaky sea salt.

BREAKFAST SALAD

SMASHED CUCUMBERS/SUMAC/
YOGURT/FRIED EGG

Makes 4 servings

This concept of a salad with your breakfast may not seem familiar to you, but to me it is. I grew up having a bit of chopped tomato and cucumber salad with every breakfast or brunch, so it's pretty standard for me. An Israeli breakfast would consist of scrambled eggs, toast, labne, olives and a chopped salad. It's a fresh and balanced way to start the day.

I don't love fresh tomatoes. Blahhhh, they're just kind of gross in my mouth. So, my breakfast salad consists of just cucumbers, unlike what I grew up on. I like the idea of smashing and tearing them to get a nice craggily edge. Use radicchio here as you would an herb and not a lettuce. Its big flavor can add just the right amount of bitterness when used this way. Granulated garlic (don't hate) is just to add a bit of savoriness to the salad without overpowering the cucumbers with fresh garlic.

THE THINGS

4 to 6 Persian cucumbers

¼ head radicchio, finely chopped

1 tbsp (4 g) chopped fresh dill

½ tsp grated ginger (grated on a microplane)

¼ tsp granulated garlic

½ tsp sumac

2 tbsp (30 ml) good olive oil

1 tbsp (15 ml) fresh lemon juice

Kosher salt

To Serve

1 cup (230 g) labne or full-fat Greek yogurt

4 fried eggs (page 30, minus the curry powder)

Sumac

Flaky sea salt

Freshly ground black pepper

THE WAY

Place the cucumbers in a resealable plastic bag and place on a cutting board. Gently crush the cucumbers with a rolling pin to break them apart. Take them out and tear them into large pieces. Place in a large bowl and add the radicchio, dill, ginger, granulated garlic, sumac, olive oil, lemon juice and kosher salt to taste. Toss gently with your hands.

Divide the cucumber salad among 4 plates with a good smear of labne and top each serving with a fried egg. Season with sumac, flaky sea salt and pepper.

HOT TIPS

- If you can't find Persian cukes, then 1 hothouse cucumber will do.

- Instead of the radicchio, try tossing a mixture of fresh herbs—such as parsley, mint and chives—into the cucumber salad.

- If it hurts your heart to smash them, you can cut the cucumbers into irregular shapes. I'd be cool with that.

CREPES

BUTTERMILK/SALTED
BROWN BUTTER/
CINNAMON SUGAR

Makes 18 to 20 crepes

Don't skip this one. I know that *crepe* sounds like something you would only eat in France, but, in fact, they're really easy to make once you've f-ed up the first two or three. Dare I say that they're easier to make than pancakes? Yes, I dare it.

The batter comes together in a blender, which means no messy bowls getting all crusty in your sink while you eat. The buttermilk gives these crepes a special tang that you wouldn't get with a regular batter. After you've made them, you fold and sauté them in salted butter and top them with cinnamon and sugar. The sweet and salty moment here is big and unforgettable.

THE THINGS

4 large eggs

3 cups (710 ml) buttermilk

½ cup (100 g) sugar, plus more for sprinkling

1 tsp vanilla bean paste or extract

½ tsp kosher salt

2 cups (250 g) all-purpose flour

3 tbsp (42 g) unsalted butter, melted

6 tbsp (84 g) salted butter, divided

Ground cinnamon, for sprinkling

THE WAY

In a blender, combine the eggs, buttermilk, sugar, vanilla bean paste and salt and blend until smooth, about 30 seconds. Add the flour and blend until just incorporated. Cover and chill for 30 minutes or up to 24 hours.

Heat a 6- to 8-inch (15- to 20.5-cm) nonstick skillet over medium-low heat. Give the batter a quick mix with a whisk. Brush the skillet lightly with melted unsalted butter and once it begins to bubble gently, pour ¼ cup (60 ml) of the batter into the pan with your weak hand and, working quickly, swirl the pan around with your dominant hand to evenly coat. Cook until lightly golden brown and the top doesn't appear wet, about 1½ minutes. Flip carefully and cook until golden brown, about another 30 seconds. Transfer to a plate and repeat, making sure to brush the pan with butter between each crepe. You can stack the crepes without them sticking.

On the plate, fold as many crepes that will fit in a large skillet in half and then in half again, working in batches. In that large skillet, heat the 2 tablespoons (28 g) of salted butter over medium heat. Once the butter foams and bubbles, add the crepes, in a single layer, to the pan. Baste the crepes in the butter until it stops foaming, is browning and smells nutty, about 1 minute. Immediately remove the pan from the heat and plate the crepes with all that butter. Sprinkle very generously with cinnamon and sugar. Repeat with the remaining crepes.

HOT TIPS

- I don't chill the batter at all sometimes and the crepes are still delicious.

- Buy good-quality salted butter. Président brand and Finlandia are great options.

FRIED EGG

CURRY/CHIVES

Makes 4 eggs

The simplest and quickest way to make an egg is to just throw it in a pan with some oil. It never fails you. It's my I'm-starving-and-need-to-put-something-in-my-body-right-now food. It's the thing my dad makes at 11:00 p.m. It's the thing that I put on my avocado toast or my bagel with cheese. The most important thing when it comes to basic fried eggs is that you get yourself some high-quality ones. You want a dark yellow, almost orange, yolk. I don't care how much I pay for my eggs as long as they are delicious. It's one of the things in my life that I've decided not to save my money on.

You can flavor the oil with so many different spices and herbs. I chose curry powder because I have a small obsession. I like a mild, yellow curry powder. Store-bought is perfectly good. This is just a nice way to heat things up and to make your tongue dance a bit. Try the eggs with other spices! Whatever your favorite may be. This is my fried curry egg . . . well, overeasy fried curry egg.

THE THINGS

Olive oil, for frying

2 tsp (4 g) mild yellow curry powder

4 large eggs

Flaky sea salt

Chopped fresh chives, for garnish

THE WAY

In a large, nonstick skillet, heat enough oil to evenly coat the bottom over medium-high heat. Add the curry powder and swirl the pan. Immediately add the eggs, one at a time. Cook until the whites are mostly set, 1½ to 2 minutes. Gently flip each egg to finish the whites. After flipping all the eggs, turn off the heat and remove them from the skillet along with all the glorious oil. Season with flaky sea salt and garnish with lots of chopped chives.

HOT TIPS

- If you shake the pan a little between each addition, the eggs will not stick together.

- Oh, baby! Definitely put this over a nice, hot bowl of grits. Like the one on page 34.

BREAKFAST TACO

SMOKED PAPRIKA EGGS/
CHEESE TORTILLA

Makes 4 servings

My way is by no means a traditional way to make a breakfast taco. This is the breakfast taco à la Danielle here. I make my eggs wrinkly, half scrambled, half omelet, with lots of smoked paprika. I like melty and crunchy bits of cheese, so instead of just adding shredded cheese to the taco, I melt and crisp it in the pan with the tortilla. It forms this crust that will make you faint.

THE THINGS

4 large eggs

Kosher salt

2 tbsp (28 g) unsalted butter

1 tbsp (15 ml) olive oil

½ tsp smoked paprika

½ tsp sweet paprika

4 corn or flour tortillas

1 cup (115 g) shredded Mexican cheese blend

1 avocado, peeled, pitted and sliced

Cholula or Frank's RedHot sauce

THE WAY

Whisk the eggs well in a bowl and season with kosher salt.

Heat a large, nonstick skillet over medium-low heat. Melt the butter and add the olive oil, then add the smoked and sweet paprika and cook until fragrant, about 30 seconds. Add the eggs to the middle of the pan. Cook, undisturbed, until the eggs begin to set, about 30 seconds. Using a rubber spatula, pull the edges of the set eggs toward the middle of the pan, allowing the raw egg to run out to the edges. Continue with this method until the eggs are mostly cooked. Flip by sheer strength and wrist power or slide the eggs onto a plate and invert them back into the pan. Immediately remove from the heat and cover to keep warm.

Heat that same large, nonstick pan over medium heat. Lay the tortillas in the pan and top with lots of shredded cheese. Cook until the tortillas are heated through and the cheese

begins to melt. Flip the tortillas. Cook, cheese side down, until it's melted and crispy, 1 to 1½ minutes. Using a spatula to release the cheese, remove the tortillas from the pan.

Divide the eggs and avocado among the tortillas. Season with salt and serve with hot sauce.

HOT TIPS

- Don't crowd the pan when making the cheesy tortillas. It's better to do it in batches, if you find that the tortillas are overlapping in the pan.

- Be sure you're using a nonstick skillet. Otherwise, you may have a mess on your hands.

- Squeeze some lime juice on that taco to brighten it up, especially if you're not into hot sauce.

GRITS

POLENTA/CRÈME
FRAÎCHE/JAM

Makes 4 servings

Grits. As I will tell you later (page 84), I didn't really know what grits were until moving to the South. I was a polenta kind of girl. But they're pretty much the same thing. Both are ground corn; polenta is made with a yellow variety, and grits with white. Grits are generally made as a savory breakfast with cheese and butter. I've already taken oatmeal savory! So, why can't I take grits (or polenta) to sweet town? It can be done.

You've been told to stay away from instant grits and polenta, and I agree with this. When preparing a dinner with a six-hour ragout, you're going to want to make the toothy, coarse polenta that you stir for 30 minutes. If you've purchased beautiful, sustainable shrimp, you're going to get the stone-ground white grits that also take 25 to 35 minutes to make. There is a time and a place for everything. But this is that moment when I lean back and grab that package of instant polenta. The more important components of this breakfast are what you top it with and how fast you can get it in the bowl and into your belly.

THE THINGS

2½ cups (590 ml) water

2½ cups (590 ml) whole milk, plus more if needed

Kosher salt

1 (9.2-oz [261-g]) package instant polenta

⅓ cup (77 g) crème fraîche

To Serve

Blackberry jam

Blackberries

Almonds

Milk or heavy cream, for drizzling

THE WAY

In a saucepan, bring the water and milk to a light boil over medium-high heat. Season with a pinch of salt. Slowly add the polenta while whisking *constantly*. Cook, stirring, until the polenta thickens, about 3 minutes. Immediately remove from the heat and stir in the crème fraîche. Add milk if it looks too thick. Divide among 4 bowls and top with the jam, berries, almonds and a drizzle of milk or cream.

HOT TIPS

- Use whichever kind of jam and fruit you have on hand. Whatever is in season is best.

- If you have the time, go ahead and prepare coarse, stone-ground polenta, following the package directions, and add crème fraîche as in the recipe at left. Coarse polenta can be made in an Instant Pot without having to stir it.

- Top with chia seeds or anything you would put on your yogurt bowl.

BAGEL

CREAM CHEESE/ALEPPO/ASPARAGUS

Makes 4 servings

I love bagels. All bagels: puffy, thin, wide, bulbous, Jerusalem style, Montreal style. I'm a fan of all spreads and toppings. I love what we've done by using bagels instead of bread in such sandwiches as the Reuben and PB&J. But what the world has done to them by dyeing them in rainbow colors and spreading cake batter–cream cheese with sprinkles all over them is an abomination. It's a disgrace to the bagel. The only food coloring that I let by is the yellow used for egg bagels, since it's a classic. The rainbow bagel trend is slowly dying and I am excited for that moment when we look back and say, "Hey, remember JNCO jeans and rainbow bagels?"

Please keep good bagels in your freezer. I keep them in resealable plastic bags and delightfully pull one out on a random Tuesday morning without having to leave the house. The day you purchase them, freeze them. When you're ready to have one, microwave on HIGH for 45 to 60 seconds, wrapped in a damp paper towel. I'm a big fan of keeping leftover veg from dinner. You can always sauté it and have it with eggs or lay it in between layers of whipped cream cheese on your toasted bagel.

THE THINGS

1 bunch asparagus, trimmed

1½ tbsp (23 ml) olive oil

1 tsp Aleppo pepper flakes

Kosher salt

Zest of 1 lemon

Whipped cream cheese (Temptee is by far my favorite)

4 bagels, sliced in half and lightly toasted

THE WAY

In a bowl, combine the asparagus with the olive oil, Aleppo and salt. Toss to coat.

Heat a grill pan or cast-iron skillet over medium heat. Grill the asparagus, turning occasionally, until lightly charred on all sides and tender, about 5 minutes. Transfer to a plate and sprinkle the lemon zest over the asparagus.

Spread a hefty layer of cream cheese on the cut sides of the bagels. Divide the asparagus among the bagels and close the sandwiches.

PASTA

THERE ARE THOSE DISHES that you try to make like your mom's but will never be like your mom's. So, I've stopped trying. Example A: Bolognese (page 50). On the other hand, when my dad makes pasta and sauce, it never tastes the same and even he can never replicate it. He can barely tell you what he's put in the sauce seconds after making it. Once I watched him carefully as he grabbed onion, celery root, cherry tomatoes, dill, turmeric, curry, black pepper, crushed coriander seeds, Aleppo, white wine, cream, Parmesan, Costco butternut squash ravioli . . . *what*??? Let me tell you, it was mind-blowing deliciousness. Thing is that my husband woke up the next morning super sick with a stomach bug. Not ravioli-related, but we decided to call this recipe Flu Sauce. I wasn't going to put this in the book. Ugh, fine, an ode to Flu Sauce is in this book (page 47).

I believe that pastas and noodles can save dinner. They don't need a ton of ingredients or even a protein to be successful. When I don't know what to make, or when I don't have a ton of energy to put a meal together, pastas are always there for me. They've never let me down. We have had a strong love affair for years on end. From the times I started cooking in college (bow ties with butter and adobo seasoning) to the times I have to feed my growing daughter (spaghetti and quick grated tomato sauce [Pomodoro, page 44]), pasta is king. As my grandpa always said, "You don't need to be hungry to eat pasta." I live by this line.

PENNE NO VODKA

PAPRIKA/SUN-DRIED TOMATOES

Makes 4 servings

This is my ultimate comfort dish. A creamy, saucy one-pot pasta with no vegetables getting in the way. This is *the* dish I make every time I have nothing specific in mind. I love penne alla vodka. It's a can't-go-wrong order at any New Jersey or New York Italian/pizza joint, which I'm sure is far from the same recipe developed by the Romans in the 1960s: a tomato and cream base, with a splash of vodka to balance the acidity of the sauce. To be honest, I don't even think those places put actual vodka in the sauce. This is not a vodka sauce, either.

The sauce appears to be tomato based, but most of the color comes from the paprika and not from the sun-dried tomatoes. Sometimes I add chicken, dried chorizo or Italian sausage before sautéing the garlic if I'm looking for a heartier dish. Either way, the penne is always cooked in chicken stock, right in the pot, because who the hell wants to do extra dishes? Cooking it right in the sauce gives the pasta flavor and the sauce body from the starch.

THE THINGS

2 tbsp (30 ml) oil from sun-dried tomatoes

4 cloves garlic, roughly chopped

1½ tbsp (10 g) sweet paprika

1 tsp smoked paprika

1 cup (110 g) roughly chopped sun-dried tomatoes, drained well (squeeze out the oil)

1 lb (455 g) dried penne pasta

4 cups (948 ml) chicken stock

Kosher salt

Freshly ground black pepper

1 cup (100 g) grated Parmesan cheese, plus more for serving

⅔ cup (160 ml) heavy cream

THE WAY

In a large, lidded sauté pan with tall sides, heat the sun-dried tomato oil over medium heat. Add the garlic and the sweet and smoked paprika and cook until fragrant, about 30 seconds. Stir in the sun-dried tomatoes and penne. Add the chicken stock and season with lots of kosher salt and pepper. Bring to a boil. Push the pasta down, making sure it isn't sticking out of the liquid. Lower the heat to low, cover and simmer, stirring occasionally, until the pasta is al dente, 8 to 10 minutes.

Add the Parmesan and cream and continue to cook, stirring, until the pasta is cooked and the sauce has thickened, about 3 minutes. Divide among 4 bowls and serve with extra Parmesan and pepper.

MACARONI & CHEESE

BOURSIN PEPPER/CAVATAPPI

Makes 4 servings

I discovered Boursin while broke and living in before-it-was-cool Bed-Stuy, Brooklyn. I had an itty-bitty tiny little stove. It was impossible to simmer sauce and boil a pot of water for pasta at the same time. Rough times. Cleanup was even worse since the sink was just big enough to wash a single dinner plate at a time. What counter space? At the time, six-dollar cheese was a splurge. On the occasional Friday night, I'd find that "fancy" cheese, Boursin, grab the most interesting pasta shapes I could find and make my one-pot mac & cheese.

When I tell you there is a "gourmet" mac & cheese that is easier to make than that boxed stuff, you may not believe me at first. But then, you'll make this recipe and you'll never go back to Kraft again. (I love Kraft Macaroni & Cheese. You can definitely keep making it.) Boursin Pepper is especially difficult to find, for some reason. I managed to locate some using the Boursin website. Yeah, it's that good.

THE THINGS

1 lb (455 g) dried cavatappi pasta

1 (5.2-oz [150-g]) package Boursin Pepper cheese

Kosher salt

Freshly ground black pepper

THE WAY

Cook the cavatappi in heavily salted boiling water according to the package directions for al dente. Reserve 1 cup (235 ml) of the cooking liquid and drain the cavatappi.

In the same pot over medium heat, melt the Boursin and the reserved cooking liquid, stirring constantly, until smooth and simmering. Add the cavatappi and stir until the sauce is thick and the pasta is covered with sauce. Season with salt. Serve with a bit more pepper.

HOT TIPS

- Save more than 1 cup (235 ml) of the pasta water and stir it in to reheat this dish.

- If the pasta and sauce become too dry, and you don't have any more pasta water, you can always stir in some milk or cream.

- You can really use *any* flavor of Boursin and your favorite pasta shape.

POMODORO

GRATED TOMATOES/PAPRIKA/GARLIC

Makes 2 servings

"Hey! We're on our way home and Zoe is hungry!" This call I get from my husband means I have exactly eight and a half minutes to get something ready for lunch. This is my life. I fill a pot with water and grab the tomatoes and my box grater. Within a few minutes, I have a quick tomato sauce that will satisfy and indulge.

Grating tomatoes is a quick way to make a tomato sauce without all the work of peeling the tomatoes. Here, I use grated tomatoes to make a pasta sauce in less than five minutes. Yup. It literally takes longer for the pasta to cook than to make this sauce. I'm using paprika to build a punchy flavor and to add a beautiful color to the oil and garlic before warming the grated tomatoes and wilting the basil. This recipe is foolproof and can be easily doubled and tripled for a larger crowd. There aren't a lot of ingredients in this recipe, so I always recommend making it when tomatoes are in season.

THE THINGS

½ lb (225 g) dried spaghetti noodles

5 Roma tomatoes, halved through stem spot

3 tbsp (45 ml) olive oil

1½ tbsp (21 g) unsalted butter

2 cloves garlic, finely sliced

2 tsp (5 g) sweet paprika

6 basil leaves

Kosher salt

Freshly ground black pepper

Chopped fresh parsley, for garnish

THE WAY

Cook the spaghetti in heavily salted boiling water according to the package instructions for al dente.

Meanwhile, make the sauce. Using the large holes of a box grater set inside a bowl, grate the cut side of the tomatoes until you're left with the skin.

In a large skillet, heat the olive oil and butter over medium heat. Add the garlic and cook until fragrant, about 30 seconds. Add the paprika and cook, stirring, for another 30 seconds. Add the grated tomatoes and cook, stirring, until the sauce heats through and just begins to bubble, about 1 minute. Using tongs, add the spaghetti straight from the boiling water to the pan with the sauce and stir to coat. Add the basil leaves and season with salt and pepper to taste. Serve garnished with the parsley.

HOT TIPS

- Add red pepper flakes while cooking the garlic and paprika, for a spicy version like an arrabbiata.

- Add a little cream to the sauce after the tomatoes come to a bubble, for a nice pink hue.

- This dish can be served at room temperature or even as a cold pasta salad. Try it with fusilli!

RAVIOLI

BUTTERNUT SQUASH
RAVIOLI/CURRY FLU
SAUCE/DILL

Makes 2 large or 4 small servings

You can count on my dad's cooking to always have curry in it. Sometimes a little pinch over a tomato salad and sometimes a ton when making chicken. It really is an incredible spice that adds warmth and flavor. To say I was skeptic of my dad's choices as he grabbed the curry powder while making a quick ravioli dish at 10:30 p.m. one night is an understatement.

The original flu sauce (check page 38 for the reason this is called flu sauce) had celery root, coriander seeds and Aleppo pepper in addition to all the ingredients below. I've cut it down for a quicker version with less stuff. The balance is perfect, so don't mess with the quantities too much. Any pumpkin or butternut squash ravioli will work here. You're looking for something that's sweet to cut the cream and spice in the sauce.

Do not change a thing about this recipe. It's perfect.

THE THINGS

1 (8-oz [225-g]) package butternut squash or pumpkin ravioli

Curry Flu Sauce

1 tbsp (15 ml) olive oil

1 tbsp (14 g) unsalted butter

½ yellow onion, thinly sliced

½ cup (75 g) cherry tomatoes, halved

Kosher salt

½ tsp ground turmeric

½ tsp curry powder

½ cup (120 ml) dry white wine

¼ cup (60 ml) chicken stock

¼ cup (60 ml) heavy cream

To Serve

¼ cup (25 g) grated Parmesan cheese

1 tbsp (4 g) chopped fresh dill

Freshly ground black pepper

THE WAY

Bring a large pot of heavily salted water to a boil. Cook the ravioli according to the package directions for al dente.

Meanwhile, prepare the curry flu sauce. In a large skillet, heat the olive oil and butter over medium heat. Add the onion and cook until softened and beginning to brown, about 5 minutes. Add the cherry tomatoes, season with salt and cook for another minute. Add the turmeric and curry powder and cook until fragrant, about 30 seconds. Increase the heat to medium-high and deglaze the pan with the white wine. Reduce by half, 2 to 4 minutes. Add the chicken stock and cream and cook until bubbly and thickening, about 2 minutes. Using a slotted spoon, transfer the ravioli to the sauce. Cook, swirling the pan, until the sauce has thickened nicely and coats the ravioli, 1 to 2 minutes. Turn off the heat and add the Parmesan, dill, more salt to taste and pepper.

Divide among plates and garnish with more Parmesan and pepper.

AGLIO E OLIO

URFA BIBER/TURMERIC/ BURRATA

Makes 4 servings

The simplest of ingredients are used to make this humble and classic pasta dish: pasta, oil, garlic and, most of the time, red pepper flakes and herbs. The variations are endless with such additions as capers, anchovies, lemon, kale, Parmesan, sun-dried tomatoes, truffle oil or even sausage. I wanted to keep things simple but punchy. This pasta can be made for a quick lunch or when you're feeling a bit snacky at 10:00 p.m.

To update and upgrade this dish, I went with turmeric and Urfa to flavor the garlic oil and topped the finished dish with creamy burrata for balance. I will use any excuse to put a ball of burrata on anything. Urfa biber is a Turkish chile pepper that's been dried and ground into flakes. It has a smoky/sweet/sour flavor, reminiscent of raisins and chocolate, that's unlike anything else. Seriously this time, make sure you have all your ingredients ready to go before putting that garlic in the oil, because it all happens real quick. I like to add a splash of balsamic vinegar on the finished dish for a beautiful sweet zing.

THE THINGS

1 lb (455 g) dried bucatini pasta

⅔ cup (160 ml) good olive oil

5 cloves garlic, thinly sliced

1 tsp Urfa biber pepper flakes

1 tsp ground turmeric

Kosher salt

1 cup (100 g) grated Parmesan cheese, plus more for serving

4 small burrata balls, for serving

Chopped fresh parsley, for serving

Freshly ground black pepper, for serving

Balsamic vinegar, to serve, optional

THE WAY

Cook the bucatini in heavily salted boiling water according to the package instructions for al dente. Drain.

Meanwhile, in a large skillet over medium heat, heat the olive oil. Add the garlic and cook until just fragrant, about 30 seconds. Add the Urfa and turmeric and cook until the oils have developed, about another 30 seconds. Add the bucatini, season with salt and toss or stir to coat. Turn off the heat and stir in the Parmesan.

Divide the pasta among 4 bowls, drizzling with whatever oil may be left in the skillet. Top with the burrata, chopped parsley, lots of black pepper and extra Parmesan. Drizzle with balsamic vinegar if you'd like.

BOLOGNESE

CHORIZO/TEMPRANILLO/RIGATONI

Makes 4 servings

It's Sunday and we're having friends over for a pasta dinner. To start: Burrata covered in my best olive oil, warmed olives and slices of dry Spanish chorizo cooked in a full bottle of red wine. Still waiting on the Bolognese, we inhaled the chorizo, using toothpicks, pretending we're having tapas in Barcelona. I had what someone would call a conniption when I realized the pot of steeped, slightly oily and red-hued wine was about to be dumped down the drain. *"There shall be no waste!"* I declared, drunkenly at this point, as I stirred the wine into the Bolognese.

Instead of simmering on the stovetop, painting your backsplash like Jackson Pollock, place that pot in a low-temperature oven. Letting the sauce braise will develop the flavors slowly, thickening and sweetening over the course of a few hours as the flavors marry. Yes. Hours. If you need more convincing, try simmering your pasta sauce in the oven to change it up a bit.

THE THINGS

2 tsp (10 ml) olive oil

8 oz (225 g) dry Spanish chorizo, sliced ¼" (6 mm) thick

3 cloves garlic, crushed

1 yellow onion, finely diced

1¼ lb (567 g) ground beef chuck (20% fat)

2½ tbsp (40 g) tomato paste

2 tbsp (32 g) sun-dried tomato paste

1 tbsp (5 g) dried oregano

Kosher salt

Freshly ground black pepper

1 (750-ml) bottle Tempranillo or Rioja wine (or whichever decent red wine you have on hand)

1 (28-oz [800-g]) can whole peeled tomatoes, drained and crushed with your hands

2 tsp (9 g) sugar

3 bay leaves

1 Parmesan rind (optional)

1 lb (455 g) dried rigatoni pasta

Parmesan cheese, for serving

Tabasco*, for serving

For the longest time, I believed Tabasco was specifically made for pasta. I imagined that every Italian home would have a small nònna serving Tabasco with spaghetti at each Sunday supper. I guess it's because I only knew of the little red and green bottle from watching my dad douse his pasta with it. It wasn't until this past year, when my friend Hollis gave me this look of, "Tabasco and spaghetti?" did I realize that Louisiana Hot Sauce might not be exclusively for pasta. It works, trust me. Is my family the only one that does this? DM me.

THE WAY

Preheat the oven to 250°F (120°C).

In a large ovenproof pot or Dutch oven, heat the olive oil over medium heat. Add the chorizo and cook, stirring occasionally, until some of the oils are released and fragrant, 2 to 3 minutes. Remove the chorizo and set aside. Add the garlic and onion and cook until softened, about 6 minutes. Add the ground beef and cook, stirring as needed, until the beef has browned, about 5 minutes. Stir in the tomato paste, sun-dried tomato paste and oregano. Cook for a minute or two, or until fragrant. Season with salt and pepper.

Deglaze the pan with the wine, taking care to scrape up all the browned bits from the bottom of the pot. Add the crushed tomatoes, sugar, bay leaves, Parmesan rind (if using) and chorizo and season gently again. Increase the heat to a light simmer, cover and transfer to the oven.

Braise for 4 hours. Remove from the oven and taste. Adjust the seasoning; discard the bay leaves and Parmesan rind.

Cook the rigatoni in heavily salted boiling water, stirring occasionally, until just al dente. Reserve 1 cup (235 ml) of pasta water and drain the pasta. Stir the rigatoni into the hot Bolognese. Add a bit of pasta water to loosen the sauce, *if needed.* Stir until the rigatoni is coated and the sauce is thick. Serve topped with grated Parmesan and Tabasco.

See photos continued on page 52.

CACIO E PEPE

GORGONZOLA/PANCETTA/
GNOCCHI

Makes 4 servings

Blue cheeses. Love them or hate them, they are the umami-est cheese along-side Parmesan. There's a stank to them that cannot be found in anything else. I haven't seen blue cheeses melted down often and it got me thinking. Why not drown gnocchi in peppery blue cheese sauce? This is not even close to your classic cacio e pepe, but it still is one, technically. As a warning: Do not test gnocchi doneness by popping one in your mouth straight out of the boiling water. #novicemovedanielle.

THE THINGS

1 lb (455 g) gnocchi

1 tbsp (15 ml) olive oil

¼ lb (115 g) pancetta, cut into ¼" (6-mm) pieces

½ cup (68 g) crumbled Gorgonzola cheese

1 cup (100 g) grated Parmesan cheese, plus more for serving

Kosher salt

Lots of freshly ground black pepper

THE WAY

Cook the gnocchi in heavily salted boiling water according to the package directions. Reserve 1 cup (235 ml) of the cooking liquid and drain the pasta.

In a large skillet, heat the olive oil over medium heat. Add the pancetta and cook, stirring occasionally, until crisp, 5 to 7 minutes. Add the Gorgonzola and about ½ cup (120 ml) of the pasta cooking liquid. Cook, stirring, until the cheese has melted and the sauce is beginning to bubble. If it is too thick, add more liquid. Add the gnocchi and Parmesan and season with salt and a lot of pepper.

Divide among 4 bowls and serve with extra Parmesan and pepper.

HOT TIPS

- If you can find guanciale, swap it in for the pancetta.

- Take it off the heat and mix with 2 eggs, transfer to a baking pan and top with more cheese, then bake at 400°F (200°C) until bubbling.

ANGEL HAIR

CARAMELIZED ONIONS/ MISO/BALSAMIC

Makes 4 servings

I've heard people say that angel hair is the garbage pasta of the pasta world. I would like to strongly disagree. I actually use capellini here, which is, just jokingly, 0.07 mm thicker than angel hair. You can use either or any other variety of thin pasta.

Making caramelized onions takes some time, but as long as you're keeping the heat low, you really can't mess it up. Just be patient, because it's where a lot of that flavor is going to come from. Everything else takes no time. I like adding miso to this for extra umami and a different kind of salt. It makes the whole dish more savory.

THE THINGS

2 tbsp (28 g) unsalted butter

2 large yellow onions, thinly sliced

Kosher salt

1 lb (455 g) dried capellini or angel hair pasta

3 tbsp (48 g) white miso

3 tbsp (45 ml) balsamic vinegar

Freshly ground black pepper

THE WAY

In a large skillet, heat the butter over medium-low heat. Add the onions and season with a pinch of salt. Cook, stirring occasionally, scraping the bottom of the skillet, until the onions are caramelized and jammy, anywhere from 35 to 45 minutes (see tip).

Meanwhile, bring a large pot of heavily salted water to a boil. Cook the pasta according to the package directions. Drain, reserving 1 cup (235 ml) of the cooking liquid.

Once the onions are dark and caramelized, stir in the miso. Cook until fragrant, about 1 minute. Deglaze the pan with the balsamic vinegar and scrape all the beautiful color up off the pan, about 30 seconds. Add ½ cup (120 ml) of the pasta cooking liquid and lower the heat to medium. Once the sauce has bubbled and thickened slightly, add the pasta and toss to coat. Taste and season with salt.

Divide among 4 bowls and season with pepper.

HOT TIPS

- How long to cook the onions depends on how thinly you cut them, the pan you're using and the amount of heat. If you find they're browning too quickly or unevenly, lower the heat to low. This will take time, so prepare the rest of your meal and stir the onions every few minutes while doing so.

- This is incredible with some chicken livers. Make the ones from page 134.

PESTO

KALE/SUNFLOWER SEEDS/
MISO

Makes 2 cups (520 g) pesto

Real pesto is simple, made with only garlic, pine nuts, basil, Parmesan (sometimes pecorino, too), salt and olive oil. Using a mortar and pestle to pound and grind the ingredients in a certain order is the only way to achieve the perfect balance and consistency. When done well, it's unlike any other pesto you've had.

This is not that recipe. I'm about to butcher some pesto and make some old Italian woman roll over in her grave. Kale gives the pesto a ton of body and a bright color without an overpowering herby flavor. I added some sunflower seeds and miso as well, to change up the flavor and to add some more umami. This pesto is good on any pasta and smothered all over some sandwiches, too.

THE THINGS

1 small bunch lacinato kale, stemmed and roughly chopped

¾ cup (175 ml) canola or grapeseed oil

1 clove garlic, crushed

1 cup (100 g) grated Parmesan cheese

¼ cup (36 g) sunflower seeds

¼ cup (35 g) pine nuts

2 tbsp (30 ml) fresh lemon juice

2 tsp (10 g) white miso

Kosher salt

THE WAY

Blanch the kale in a large pot of heavily salted boiling water, until bright green and slightly wilted, 30 to 45 seconds. Immediately drain in a colander and rinse with cold water to stop the cooking. Drain and squeeze out as much of the water as you can.

Place the kale and all the other ingredients, except for the salt, in a food processor and blend on low speed until well chopped and almost creamy. The pesto does not have to be totally smooth. Taste and adjust the seasoning with salt.

Store in the fridge, well covered, for up to 2 days. Toss a few tablespoons with any shape of pasta.

HOT TIPS

- Grill some chicken and smother the pesto all over it.

- In the summer, top beautiful sliced tomatoes with it.

- My favorite pasta to use for this pesto is actually Israeli couscous.

- Instead of the 1 cup (100 g) of Parmesan, try ½ cup (50 g) of Parmesan and ½ cup (50 g) of Pecorino Romano, for a funkier taste.

RAMEN

TAHINI/SUMAC/PINE NUTS

Makes 4 servings

Everyone growing up in my hometown of Cresskill has eaten at Hanami, a Japanese and Chinese restaurant right in the middle of town. Until this day, it's the only non-pizza or -bagel place in town.* It would serve cold or warm sesame noodles that I still dream about. We would *always* order it. It was also always in the leftovers section at my friend Jess's house, her family's fridge staple.

There is something about a noodle smothered in tahini that is irresistible. Slurping is totally okay when eating ramen noodles and this gives me a good excuse to eat loudly without my husband getting pissy with me. I tell him that it's ramen tradition. I have all of these things in my pantry at all times and this is very easy to throw together. I love the sumac and pine nuts for a contrast of tang and crunch to the creamy, nutty sauce.

THE THINGS

⅔ cup (160 g) tahini

1 clove garlic

2 tbsp (30 ml) soy sauce

1 tbsp (15 ml) rice vinegar

1 tsp light brown sugar

Kosher salt

½ to ⅔ cup (120 to 160 ml) water

2 (3.7-oz [104-g]) packages dried ramen noodles

1 avocado, peeled, pitted and thinly sliced

1 Persian cucumber, thinly sliced

2 scallions, thinly sliced

¼ cup (35 g) toasted pine nuts

Black sesame seeds

Sumac

THE WAY

In a blender, puree the tahini, garlic, soy sauce, rice vinegar, brown sugar, salt and ½ cup (120 ml) of the water until smooth. Add more water if the sauce is too thick. It should be a bit thicker than pancake batter.

Cook the ramen according to the package directions, discarding any spice mix that may have come with it. Drain, then toss with the dressing.

Divide the noodles among 4 bowls, top with avocado, cucumber, scallions and pine nuts and garnish with a good amount of black sesame seeds and sumac.

*Not factual. I haven't eaten in Cresskill, New Jersey, since 2005.

PASTINA

SAUSAGE/PEAS/ZA'ATAR

Makes 4 servings

Pastina is more than the only thing I can manage to keep down when I'm sick. It's filed under "Most Comforting Bowls" in my brain. I remember my mom making me bowls of silky pastina after school on super-cold New Jersey days with simply butter and salt. Pastina is one of those pasta shapes you totally forget about until you get to the grocery store and you see that box among the large pasta shapes. But it's more than just those tiny little stars. They come in other shapes, such as farfalline, ditalini, risi and quadretti. I've chosen to use acini di pepe, which translates to "seeds of pepper." They resemble pearl couscous but are smaller.

I wanted to make pastina exciting by treating it like a regular pasta. The whole idea behind this dish was to have a little bit of each component in every bite, which makes it easy to just shovel it in your mouth mindlessly. Be sure to break up the sausage real well and allow it to crisp up nice. The za'atar adds a different flavor to the otherwise classic pasta with sausage and peas. It's not overpowering at all. Just has you going, "Huh. What is that flavor?"

THE THINGS

½ cup (125 g) acini di pepe pasta

⅔ cup (87 g) frozen peas

1 tbsp (15 ml) olive oil

⅔ lb (303 g) mild Italian sausage meat

½ cup (50 g) grated Parmesan cheese

1 tbsp (7 g) za'atar

Kosher salt

Freshly ground black pepper

THE WAY

Bring a large pot of heavily salted water to a boil. Cook the acini di pepe according to the package directions. Add the frozen peas to the boiling water in the last minute of cooking. Drain, reserving 1 cup (235 ml) of the cooking liquid.

Meanwhile, in a large skillet, heat the olive oil over medium heat. Add the Italian sausage to the pan in crumbles. Cook, undisturbed, until nicely browned, 2 to 3 minutes. Break up the meat into smaller pieces with a wooden spoon. Cook, stirring occasionally and continuing to break up the sausage, until nicely browned and cooked through, another 5 minutes. Add ½ cup (120 ml) of the pasta cooking liquid to the pan and scrape the bottom to release all the tasty bits. Add the acini di pepe and peas. Bring to a simmer while stirring. Add the Parmesan and za'atar. Cook, stirring constantly, until you have a glossy sauce, about 1 minute. Add more cooking liquid, if needed. Taste and season with salt and pepper.

Divide among 4 serving bowls and serve immediately.

TURF & SURF

HERE ARE THE HEAVY HITTERS. The "this-is-what's-for-dinner" chapter. Just because you work in the culinary world, doesn't mean that it's easy to get dinner on the table for your family. It's almost harder, because you've been dealing with food all day. Even when writing a cookbook, I'd have friends say, "Nice! So, dinner is basically what you tested that day." Not exactly. When testing for a cookbook, you either make a smaller batch at first to check the flavor profiles, or you make a big batch and it's a total failure, or you make the dish to photograph it and have messed with it so much that it becomes inedible. So, after cooking and testing all day, there still needs to be dinner at 5:00.

I look for quick-cooking or easy-prep-type meals during the weekdays. It's boring to make the same things over and over even though it requires no brain work. My mom would make a rotation of schnitzel, "white" steak, Bolognese, *batata sofrito* (fried chicken and potatoes), beef with string beans and pita pizza. I'm not sure how no one got tired of it. This is why I tweaked or upgraded these recipes from our originals for a bit more excitement. Makes it feel like something new. Some of these recipes you will be able to adapt to make your own go-tos. Try adding red wine and chorizo to a quick weekday meat sauce or jazz up your Monday night grilled chicken with a spice mix (for example, shawarma spice, page 159). Use these recipes as guidelines and adjust your usual suspects. These recipes are simple enough to add to your repertoire but bold enough to keep you excited!

CHICKEN & POTATOES

INSTANT POT SHREDDED
CHICKEN/MASHED POTATOES/
CUMIN TZATZIKI

Makes 4 servings

My daughter didn't start getting her teeth until she was almost eleven months old (which is late). We loved her gummy smile, but I had to make her food that she was able to swallow without chewing.

I used to make Greek chicken and potatoes in the oven every week because it was something my husband grew up eating often. Needless to say, it got super-boring. After seeing how much my daughter loved it, and not to mention the ease in which she was able to eat it with her gummy, toothless smile, I knew this was a recipe that needed tweaking. I didn't want the flavor to change much, just the method in which I was cooking it. That was enough to make us more enthused about chicken and potato night.

I fell for the Instant Pot craze. I was just in the market for a pressure cooker, but here we are. The chicken comes out super-soft and stringy with an intense lemon sauce, a.k.a. "juice." I've learned that it's the perfect way to make shredded chicken because the pressure cooker doesn't dry it out and cooks it just enough. The potatoes cook along with the chicken and I just easily mash them as I plate them, no extra work here. And how about this: Don't bother salting and squeezing out the water from the cucumbers for the tzatziki when using thick, full-fat yogurt. Say it with me now: "No. Extra. Work. Here." Weeknight dinner slam dunk.

THE THINGS

2 lb (905 g) boneless, skinless chicken thighs

⅔ cup (160 ml) fresh lemon juice

⅔ cup (160 ml) chicken stock

1½ tbsp (23 ml) olive oil, plus more for serving

1 tbsp (5 g) dried oregano

1 lb (455 g) small, white baby potatoes, halved

Kosher salt

Freshly ground black pepper

2 Persian cucumbers

1½ cups (345 g) full-fat Greek yogurt (5% Fage brand works best)

1½ tbsp (23 ml) fresh lemon juice

¼ tsp ground cumin

¼ tsp garlic powder

HOT TIPS

- That cucumber salad from page 26 will work real nice here as a side salad.

- Shred the chicken and mix with the "juice" for a cold chicken salad.

- If you don't care for potatoes, try this on top of some cooked wild rice.

THE WAY

In an Instant Pot, combine the chicken thighs, lemon juice, chicken stock, olive oil and oregano, neatly arranging the chicken in a single layer along the bottom so that each thigh is a tight little package. Place the potatoes, cut side down, in a single layer on top of the chicken. Season with salt and lots of pepper.

Set the Instant Pot to pressure cook on HIGH for 27 minutes. Allow the pressure to release naturally.

To prepare the tzatziki, using the smaller holes on a box grater, grate the cucumbers, skin and all, into a large bowl. Add the yogurt, lemon juice, cumin, garlic powder and salt to taste and mix well.

When serving, slightly mash the potatoes into the bottom of a bowl, top with the chicken, shred it slightly, and top with the "juice" from the pot and tzatziki. Drizzle with a little good-quality olive oil.

See photos continued on page 68.

STEAK

SHABU-SHABU CUT/ CHILE-LIME BUTTER

Makes 4 servings with extra butter

I have forever been going to Asian grocery stores and gawking at the beautifully sliced shabu-shabu meats. If you've ever gone for hotpot, you've gotten a tray of super-thinly sliced beef or pork that you poach in a bubbling broth. It's such a beautiful thing to see how thinly meat can be sliced. When I see it, I just want to throw it into a super-hot pan and get some charring going on. And so I did, and so it was delicious.

This recipe is the definition of minute steak. After making the compound butter, it literally takes one (okay, maybe two) minutes to put together. I love this hot, sweet, peppery, tangy compound butter, but any good, flavored butter will work here. I am able to find shabu-shabu beef at my Asian grocery store. If you can't find it, any thinly cut steak will do the job; you'll just want to adjust the cooking time accordingly.

THE THINGS

8 tbsp (112 g) unsalted butter, at room temperature

1 clove garlic, grated on a microplane

½ to ¼ tsp ancho chile powder

1 tsp Urfa biber

Zest of 1 lime

1½ tsp (8 ml) fresh lime juice

1½ tsp (10 g) honey

Kosher salt

Canola oil

1 lb (455 g) shabu-shabu-style New York strip steak

Freshly ground black pepper

THE WAY

In a bowl, mix together the butter, garlic, ancho chile, Urfa, lime zest and juice, honey and a few good pinches of salt until combined.

In a large skillet, heat about 1 tablespoon (15 ml) of canola oil over medium-high. Season the steak with salt and black pepper. In batches if needed, cook the steak, undisturbed, until well browned, about 1½ minutes. Add 1 to 2 tablespoons (15 to 30 g) of the prepared butter and flip the steak, then cook while swirling the pan for another 30 seconds. Add more oil to the skillet after each batch.

Serve immediately with extra prepared butter.

HOT TIPS

- Place any remaining prepared butter on a large piece of plastic wrap and roll it up into a log. This will keep in the fridge for 2 to 3 days. I usually make the butter a day ahead of time to have dinner together in 3 minutes.

- Excellent on top of salads.

- Use this butter to toss with steamed or grilled vegetables, for a new and exciting side.

MEATBALLS

HARISSA/MOZZARELLA/SANDWICH
OPTIONAL

Makes about 15 meatballs

There's an amazing Italian sandwich shop that has stuck around over the years near my hometown. It serves the most incredible Italian subs filled with freshly sliced meats piled super-high with finely shredded iceberg. Every third week, I'd get the meatball sub. Mostly to hear the old man behind the counter say "meatbawwl," but also because it was delicious.

Meatballs are not that complicated or time consuming to make, I promise. Once you have the ingredients prepped, they come together really quickly. They don't have to be something you make on Sundays only. I don't bother searing the balls prior to putting them in the sauce, which cuts down on some steps. They're perfectly flavorful and juicy even still. These have a good kick from the harissa, which elevates your basic ball. I enjoy a sandwich, so I put the meatballs into one. They're great on their own or even smashed in a pita.

THE THINGS

1½ lb (680 g) ground chuck

1 small yellow onion, grated on large holes of box grater

⅓ cup (33 g) kalamata olives, pitted and roughly chopped

½ cup (60 g) bread crumbs

1½ tsp to 1 tbsp (8 to 15 g) harissa

1½ tsp (3 g) Italian seasoning

1½ tsp (9 g) Diamond brand kosher salt

Freshly ground black pepper

Sauce

2 tbsp (30 ml) olive oil

8 cloves garlic, roughly chopped

2 tbsp (32 g) tomato paste

1 to 2 tbsp (15 to 30 g) harissa

1 tbsp (6 g) Italian seasoning

1½ tsp (4 g) sweet paprika

1 (28-oz [800-g]) can crushed tomatoes

Kosher salt

Freshly ground black pepper

To Serve

Italian sub roll, optional

Slices of provolone or fresh mozzarella, optional

THE WAY

In a large bowl, combine the beef, grated onion, olives, bread crumbs, harissa, Italian seasoning, salt and some pepper. Portion out and roll into 15 meatballs, about ¼ cup (65 g) each, and set on a parchment-lined baking sheet.

In a large, lidded sauté pan with tall sides, heat the olive oil over medium heat. Add the garlic and cook until fragrant, about 30 seconds. Add the tomato paste, harissa to taste, Italian seasoning and paprika. Cook until pasty, about 30 seconds. Add the crushed tomatoes and bring to a gentle boil. Season generously with salt and pepper. Transfer the meatballs to the sauce. Cover and cook, swirling the pan occasionally, until the meatballs are cooked through, 25 to 30 minutes.

Optional: Heat your broiler to HIGH. Slice the sub roll in half and place slices of cheese on both cut halves. Broil on a rimmed baking sheet until the cheese is melted and bubbling, 1 to 3 minutes. Smash a few meatballs on one side of the sub roll, close the sandwich and enjoy.

CHEESE-BURGER

CUMIN/ÜBER-THIN
GROUND CHUCK/BASIC
WHITE BREAD

Makes 2 half sandwiches

I once had an amazing folded cheeseburger in New York City from a spot called Miznon. The Israeli chef who owns it, Eyal Shani, is simply a culinary genius. This burger is inspired by the folded cheeseburger at Miznon . . . and the Big Mac. You read that correctly. A burger is not something to be messed with. I'm not a fan of a million toppings ranging from onion rings to whole grilled cheeses. I just barely accept bacon on my burger (unless it's the Bacon King from Burger King . . . I have a fast-food problem). Keep it simple, stupid. Meat, onions, pickles, lettuce (only shredded iceberg, none of that romaine crap), and a version of a special sauce.

The key to this burger is the technique. The patty is extra thin, which allows for more surface area to brown and crisp. Now, here's some bad news: Unless you have multiple griddles, or four big cast-iron skillets, you're going to have trouble making this for a crowd. The burgers are 8 inches (21 cm) wide before folding, so if you're planning on making this for you and your boo, you'll be able to swing it. Don't try making eight of these for all your friends, otherwise you're going to have to make them in batches (see first tip). This recipe is so good that I'm not even sorry for it.

THE THINGS

⅔ lb (303 g) ground chuck (20% fat)

2 tbsp (28 g) unsalted butter, at room temperature

2 slices soft sandwich bread, such as potato bread or straight-up Wonder Bread

Mayonnaise

Ketchup

Yellow mustard

¼ tsp ground cumin

Kosher salt

Freshly ground black pepper

4 slices American cheese

Red onions, sliced paper thin on a mandoline

Finely shredded iceberg lettuce

Bread-and-butter pickle slices

HOT TIPS

- Okay, fine, get a pound (455 g) of ground chuck and make the burgers ¼ pound (about 115 g) each. You'll have four bitties and more servings. Roll them out to ¼ inch (6 mm) thick still.

- Have the toppings ready to go before you start cooking the burgers.

- Use your recipe for special sauce here, but I'm too lazy and just squirt each condiment straight onto the bread.

THE WAY

Divide the meat into 2 equal parts and do not ball up; leave it loose. Place 1 portion on the bottom half of a large sheet of parchment paper, fold the parchment in half and roll out the meat to ¼ inch (6 mm) thick and about 8 inches (21 cm) in diameter. Do the same with the other portion, keeping them in the parchment until ready to cook.

Heat a cast-iron griddle or cast-iron skillet over medium-high heat until hot. Spread the butter on one of the bread slices and toast, butter side down, until golden brown, 1 to 2 minutes. Do not toast the other side.

Slice the bread in half on the diagonal. Dress the side that has not been toasted with a bit of mayo, ketchup and mustard. A little goes a long way with each.

Season the beef patties with a sprinkle of cumin, lots of kosher salt and pepper. Working in batches if needed, place the patties on the griddle, seasoned side down, and give each a little press with a spatula. Season the other side with a bit more cumin, salt and pepper. Cook, undisturbed, until the outer edges are browned and the meat has basically cooked through to the top, about

3 minutes. There may be some redness left, but the residual heat will take care of that after you fold it. Place 2 slices of American cheese on half of each patty and fold the patty in half. Transfer each folded patty to the bread and top with onions, lettuce and pickles. Close the sandwich and eat immediately.

See photos continued on page 76.

SALMON

HARISSA/SOY/
CASTELVETRANO OLIVES

Makes 4 servings

If you make salmon on a regular basis, you know how quickly it can come together. But if you make it on a regular basis, like us, you also stop getting excited for salmon night. When I ask my husband what we should make for dinner and he says "salmon," it almost sounds like a sigh and a shrug. Get excited, my friends, because this is the salmon recipe that will bring back the love. And if you don't normally make salmon at home, this is a great recipe to get you started. It's pretty foolproof.

The trick with salmon is to cook it high and quick or low and super-slow. You can also cure it, but that's for another time. I broil mine on high for six to seven minutes and it's totally ready. A spicy, sweet and salty marinade/sauce comes together real quick with a match made in heaven: harissa, honey and soy sauce. I don't bother pulling out a knife for this recipe because I believe that olives taste better when torn. All those rough edges just make it. I use Castelvetrano olives, which are beautifully bright green and have good meaty flesh that holds up to the broiler heat. Serve this with wild rice or farro.

THE THINGS

3 tbsp to ⅓ cup (45 to 80 g) harissa (depending on how spicy the harissa is)

2 tbsp (40 g) honey

3 tbsp (45 ml) soy sauce

2 tsp (10 ml) sesame oil

2 tsp (5 g) black sesame seeds

Kosher salt

4 skinless salmon fillets (5 to 6 oz [140 to 170 g] each), any pin bones removed

1½ cups (270 g) Castelvetrano olives, pitted and torn in half

THE WAY

In a bowl, whisk together the harissa, honey, soy sauce, sesame oil, sesame seeds and salt. Transfer half of the mixture into a resealable plastic bag and add the salmon fillets to the bag. Seal and very gently move the bag around to cover the salmon with the marinade. Set in the fridge to marinate for 25 to 30 minutes.

With the oven rack in the upper third position, preheat the broiler to HIGH.

On a rimmed baking sheet, spread out the olives in a single layer, making sure they are not spread out too much. Remove the salmon fillets from the marinade and lay over the olives, leaving 1 inch (2.5 cm) of space between the fillets. The salmon should not be touching the baking sheet. Discard the bagged marinade.

Broil on high for 6 to 7 minutes, basting every 2 to 3 minutes with the reserved marinade, or until the salmon is charred and cooked to medium rare. Serve with the remaining reserved marinade as a sauce.

HOT TIPS

- Store-bought harissa can vary from very mild to very hot. Be sure to taste it beforehand, so that you know how much spice you're adding.

- If you can't find Castelvetrano olives, use any other mild, salt-brined green olives.

MEAT LOAF

BAHARAT/DRIED
CHERRIES/OLIVES/
SILAN SOY GLAZE

Makes 8 servings

Meat loaf does not need to be boring, dry or wrapped in bacon. My mom used to make meat loaf, but I found that I never, ever made it for my family. I think that in this day and age, meat loaf needs a facelift because it peaked in the 1950s. Yup, no ketchup in this recipe.

For me, it starts and ends with the glaze. It's sweet and sour, but balanced. This is what takes the place of ketchup. Total upgrade already. But then the addition of yogurt, olives, dried cherries, pistachios and baharat really bring it home. I make my own Baharat Mix (page 159) but store-bought is totally fine, too. Enjoy with a bit of yogurt and za'atar and you have yourself a Middle Eastern meat loaf.

THE THINGS

Glaze

⅓ cup (90 g) tomato paste

2 tbsp (30 ml) silan (date syrup)

1 tbsp (15 ml) balsamic vinegar

1 tbsp (15 ml) soy sauce

Meat Loaf Mixture

1 tbsp (15 ml) olive oil

1 medium carrot, grated on large holes of a box grater

1 small yellow onion, grated on large holes of a box grater

4 cloves garlic, roughly chopped

2 lb (905 g) ground chuck (20% fat)

1 tbsp (8 g) Baharat Mix (page 159)

⅓ cup (77 g) full-fat Greek yogurt, plus more for serving

¼ cup (31 g) pistachios

⅓ cup (40 g) dried tart cherries

⅓ cup (33 g) pitted green olives

¼ cup (28 g) plain bread crumbs

2 large eggs

1 tbsp (19 g) Diamond brand kosher salt

Freshly ground black pepper

Za'atar, for serving

THE WAY

Prepare the glaze. In a small bowl, combine the tomato paste, silan, balsamic vinegar and soy sauce.

Preheat the oven to 350°F (180°C) and place the rack in the middle position.

Prepare the meat loaf mixture. In a large skillet, heat the olive oil over medium heat. Add the carrot, onion and garlic and cook until softened and most of the water has evaporated, about 8 minutes. Turn off the heat and allow the mixture to cool slightly.

In a large bowl, combine the cooled carrot mixture, ground beef, baharat, 2 tablespoons (30 ml) of the glaze, yogurt, pistachios, cherries, olives, bread crumbs, eggs, salt and pepper. **Note: The meat loaf mixture can be made a day ahead.**

To bake, form a 9 x 5–inch (23 x 12.5–cm) loaf on a foil-covered rimmed baking sheet. Alternatively, place in a standard loaf pan for a more uniform meat loaf. Spread some glaze over all of the loaf, sides included. Bake for 1 hour, reglazing the loaf at 40 minutes, 50 minutes and then 55 minutes. Pull it out of the oven as soon as the internal temperature reads 155°F (68°C). If baking it straight out of the fridge, be sure that it comes up to temperature, which may take a bit longer than an hour.

Let it rest for at least 15 minutes before slicing and serving with additional yogurt (thin with water, if desired) and za'atar.

PAILLARD

TURMERIC/CUMIN/RADISH & CABBAGE SUMAC SLAW

Makes 4 servings

Paillard: the French schnitzel without the coating. Not really, but it sounds good. It merely means that you've beaten the crap out of a piece of meat until it's thin, tender and can cook quickly.

Boneless, skinless chicken breast could possibly be the most boring thing out there. It's bland, blah chicken. But I find that if you pound it out, cover it in spices and top it with a tangy slaw, then it sure as hell ain't so bad. When you flash fry chicken breast like this, there's not much time for it to dry out. I love this recipe for a chicken sandwich.

THE THINGS

Slaw

¼ cup (60 ml) olive oil

3 tbsp (45 ml) lemon juice

1½ tsp (10 g) agave nectar or 1 tsp honey

2 tsp (5 g) sumac

½ tsp ground white pepper

Kosher salt

1 medium savoy cabbage, finely shredded on a mandoline

2 medium radishes, thinly sliced on a mandoline

Chicken

4 boneless, skinless chicken breasts

Canola oil, for frying

2 tbsp (14 g) turmeric

1 tsp ground cumin

Kosher salt

To Serve

Parmesan cheese

Slather of mayonnaise

THE WAY

Prepare the slaw. In a small bowl, whisk together the olive oil, lemon juice, agave, sumac, white pepper and salt. Toss with the cabbage and radishes. If you like a crisp slaw instead of a wilted one, toss in the dressing just before serving.

Prepare the chicken. Butterfly the chicken by placing it on a cutting board and, with your hand flat on top, slice into one side of the breast, taking care not to slice the entire way through. Open the breast, cover with a large resealable bag and pound the breast with a flat mallet or rolling pin until about ¼ inch (6 mm) thick.

In a large skillet, heat about 1 tablespoon (15 ml) of oil over medium-high heat. Season the cutlets with the turmeric, cumin and salt. Cook the cutlets in batches, so as to not crowd the skillet, until golden brown, about 3 minutes. Flip and cook until cooked through, about another minute. Repeat with the remaining cutlets.

Serve the slaw over the chicken. Shave some Parmesan over the slaw and with a slather of mayo on the side of the plate.

HOT TIPS

- Keep the cutlets warm on a rack set over a rimmed baking sheet in a 200°F (90°C) oven, so everyone can have warm chicken at the same time, since you're frying them in batches.

- If you're real lazy, you can butterfly the chicken ahead of time and freeze the flattened breasts individually in resealable plastic bags. Defrost in the fridge overnight or transfer them to the fridge in the morning when you'll cook them for dinner.

SHRIMP & GRITS

CURRY/CREAM CHEESE GRITS

Makes 4 servings

I never understood why people loved grits. It's just this pasty white, flavorless goop that used to make me think of basic cream of wheat (barf). Then, I moved to Atlanta. Sitting in a more upscale restaurant, I noticed "pimiento grits" on the menu and said to myself, "If I try these and don't get it, then maybe I'm the crazy one." Needless to say that it was not the goopy mush I would get up north in Jersey; this was creamy, cheesy deliciousness.

This take on shrimp and grits takes you over to the world of my quick curries. Yes, you can make a super-quick, punchy curry with minimal ingredients. I'm sure that I am not the first to tell you this. The cream cheese grits are perfect with the curry: not too strong, but creamy as hell.

Tidbit: My mom eats grits with maple syrup . . . is this a thing? Or can I make fun of her for it?

THE THINGS

3 cups (710 ml) water

1 cup (235 ml) whole milk

Kosher salt

1 cup (155 g) uncooked white grits

½ cup (115 g) cream cheese

Freshly ground black pepper

2 tbsp (28 g) unsalted butter

2 cloves garlic, grated on a microplane

2 tbsp (30 g) red curry paste

1 tsp mild curry powder

1 (14-oz [400-g]) can coconut milk

2 tsp (10 ml) Asian fish sauce

1½ lb (680 g) large shrimp, peeled and deveined

Fresh cilantro leaves, for garnish

THE WAY

In a large saucepan, bring the water, milk and a healthy pinch of salt to a boil over medium-high heat. Gradually whisk in the grits until smooth. Lower the heat to low, cover and cook, stirring occasionally, until creamy. Depending on the brand of grits, this can take between 10 and 25 minutes.

Remove from the heat and stir in the cream cheese. Season with additional salt and pepper to taste.

Meanwhile, in a large skillet, heat the butter over medium-high heat. Cook the garlic, red curry paste and curry powder, stirring, until fragrant, about 30 seconds. Add the coconut milk and fish sauce, stirring, and continue to cook until it begins to simmer. Add the shrimp and cook, swirling the skillet occasionally, until just pink and opaque, about 4 minutes.

Taste and season with salt, but be careful because most curry pastes are already salty!

Serve the shrimp and sauce over the grits. Garnish with cilantro and additional pepper.

HOT TIPS

- If the grits become too thick, stir in some milk to loosen them up.
- I use Mae Ploy brand red curry paste.
- Put the Kimchi Pulled Pork (page 87) on these grits instead of the curry shrimp.

PULLED PORK

KIMCHI/GOCHUJANG/
SORGHUM/SOY SAUCE

Makes 6 to 8 servings

As much as I would love to take credit for fusing Korean flavors with southern barbecue, I obviously can't. The two just work so incredibly well together. A lot of the techniques are very similar: slow-roasting pork in a sweet barbecue sauce or marinating and grilling the meat over high heat. Slaws, pickles and ferments—all very similar. The ingredients change, but the techniques remain. I jump at any opportunity to make slow-cooker pulled pork because it's easy, cheap, feeds a crowd and I get to use my Costco membership to get a nice butt—of pork, that is.

This recipe reminds me of North Carolina–style pulled pork because it's got a nice vinegar kick plus the fermented flavor of the kimchi. Sweet, tangy and a bit spicy, the pork is perfectly delicious on its own. If you must . . . serve with fresh slaw, grits, soft flour tortillas or brioche buns for sandwiches.

THE THINGS

3 cloves garlic, grated on a microplane

1 (3" [7.5-cm]) piece peeled ginger, grated on a microplane

⅓ cup (80 g) ketchup

3 tbsp (45 ml) soy sauce

2 tbsp (30 g) gochujang (Korean chili paste)

2 tbsp (30 g) dark brown sugar

1½ tbsp (23 ml) rice vinegar

1 tbsp (20 g) sorghum syrup or honey

1 tbsp (15 ml) sesame oil

1 tsp mild yellow mustard powder

1 (3-lb [1.5-kg]) Boston butt (boneless pork shoulder), cut into 3 large pieces

Kosher salt

Freshly ground black pepper

1½ tbsp (12 g) cornstarch

1½ tbsp (23 ml) water

1½ cups (225 g) cabbage kimchi, chopped

THE WAY

In a slow cooker, whisk together the garlic, ginger, ketchup, soy sauce, gochujang, brown sugar, rice vinegar, sorghum, sesame oil and mustard powder. Add the pork and coat with the sauce. Season with lots of kosher salt and pepper. Cook on low for 8 to 10 hours.

Transfer the pork to a large dish and shred with 2 forks.

In a small bowl, combine the cornstarch and water, stir into the sauce and turn the cooker to high. Cook the sauce, stirring occasionally, until thickened, about 10 minutes. Return the pork to the slow cooker along with the chopped kimchi and combine with the sauce. Lower the slow cooker setting to WARM and serve.

HOT TIPS

- Pickles. This pulled pork loves anything pickled or fermented.

- Try with the slaw from the Paillard (page 83).

- Make this an overnight slow-cooker meal to have ready to take to lunch with you.

PORK CHOPS

URFA PICO DE GALLO/
TAHINI

Makes 4 servings

Okay, so pork isn't kosher, if you didn't know. But in Israel, there are a small handful of joints that serve thinly sliced pork chops as "white steak," flash grilled over charcoal, then stuffed in a pita and covered in tahini sauce. After moving to the United States, my mom started cooking more and more "white steak" since it was so easy to find. She would sprinkle it with cumin and white pepper, quickly sear it in a hot pan and serve it with Israeli salad.

This cooks up super-quick. It literally takes two minutes on each side and it's done. I serve it with tahini, totally raw, and fresh Urfa pico de gallo. Urfa, or Urfa biber, is a mild dried Turkish chile pepper with notes of smoky raisins. There really is no substitute!

THE THINGS

6 to 8 Roma tomatoes, finely diced

2 cloves garlic, grated on a microplane

⅛ red onion, finely diced

2 tbsp (5 g) finely chopped fresh cilantro

2 tbsp (30 ml) fresh lime juice

2 tsp (5 g) Urfa biber

Kosher salt

1½ tbsp (11 g) ground cumin

1½ tsp (3 g) ground white pepper

8 thinly sliced boneless pork chops, about ¼" (6 mm) thick

Canola oil, for frying

Tahini, to serve

Lime wedges, to serve

THE WAY

Prepare the Urfa pico de gallo. In a bowl, combine the tomatoes, garlic, red onion, cilantro, lime juice, Urfa and salt to taste.

Prepare the pork. In a small bowl, combine the cumin and white pepper. Season both sides of each chop generously with the spice mixture and salt.

Heat enough canola oil to thinly coat the bottom of a large skillet over medium-high heat. In batches, so as to not crowd the pan, add the chops and cook undisturbed for 2 minutes, until browned. Flip and cook for another 1½ to 2 minutes.

Serve with tahini, lime wedges and the Urfa pico de gallo.

CHICKEN SOUP

HOMINY/POBLANO/
CHEEZ-ITS

Makes 4 servings

Thing 1: Living in New York City, it was extremely easy to find a good chicken soup at every little hole-in-the-wall diner. I never bothered making it at home on those cold days when all I wanted to do after work was sit in front of the TV watching *Deadliest Catch* with a bowl of chicken soup. Preferably with rice, but noodles will do, too.

Thing 2: Pozole. A traditional Mexican soup made with hominy, pork or chicken, shredded cabbage, radish, avocado and a lot of lime. There are a ton of versions, but I had fallen in love with a green pozole from a small spot here in Atlanta.

My chicken-pozole hybrid soup is the only right thing on a wrong day. It's just as much about the toppings as it is about the soup itself. I usually top my soups with something crunchy to give it contrast. One day I literally had nothing but Cheez-It crackers in my pantry; I decided to give it a go. Now, it's the first thing I grab when sitting down with a bowl of soup. Don't add too many at the same time because they get soggy quickly, which is why I just keep the whole box close by.

THE THINGS

1 yellow onion, roughly chopped

7 cloves garlic

1 poblano pepper, stemmed and seeded, roughly chopped

1 (4-oz [115-g]) can green chile peppers

1½ tsp (4 g) ground cumin

1½ tsp (4 g) ground coriander

1 tsp ground oregano

2 tbsp (30 ml) apple cider vinegar

4 cups (948 ml) chicken stock

2 tbsp (30 ml) olive oil

Kosher salt

Freshly ground black pepper

2 lb (905 g) boneless, skinless chicken thighs

1 (25-oz [708-g]) can hominy, drained

To Serve

Cheez-It crackers

Sliced avocado

Thinly sliced radish

Fresh cilantro leaves

Lime wedges

THE WAY

In a blender, puree the onion, garlic, poblano, green chiles, cumin, coriander, oregano, apple cider vinegar and chicken stock until fairly smooth.

In a heavy-bottomed pot, heat the olive oil over high heat. Add the puree and season with salt and black pepper to taste. Add the chicken thighs and hominy and bring to a boil. Once boiling, skim off any foam that has accumulated at the top. Lower the heat to low, cover and simmer for at least 1 hour and up to 3 hours.

Remove the chicken and shred. Return it back to the soup. Serve the soup topped with Cheez-Its, avocado, radish, cilantro and lime.

FISH & CHIPS

HAWAIJ/SALT & VINEGAR
CHIPS

Makes 4 servings

Hawaij, a Yemenite spice mixture, is usually used to flavor soups, stews and coffee. The combination and quantity of spices changes depending on which family is making it, but it's generally turmeric, cumin, cardamom and black pepper. It's a great combination and works extremely well on fish with something vinegary to cut through the spice. How about some classic salt and vinegar chips? No question.

The fish should be liberally covered with hawaij. Use any meaty, fresh white fish here. You either love or hate salt and vinegar chips; there is no in-between. So, if you really hate them, just don't eat them with the fish. Try serving it with asparagus (page 37) or green beans (page 106). It could also really be delicious over the Caesar salad (page 110). Better yet, serve with chimichurri (page 122).

THE THINGS

2½ tsp (6 g) ground turmeric

1½ tsp (4 g) ground cumin

1 tsp ground coriander

¼ tsp ground cardamom

¼ tsp freshly ground black pepper

4 (5- to 6-oz [140- to 170-g]) skinless, boneless halibut, mahi-mahi or cod fillets

1½ tbsp (23 ml) canola oil

Kosher salt

Salt and vinegar potato chips (preferably Lay's)

THE WAY

In a small bowl, combine the turmeric, cumin, coriander, cardamom and pepper to create the hawaij blend.

Generously rub the fillets with the hawaij on all sides. If you have the time, let the spice-rubbed fish rest for 30 minutes in the fridge. But it'll be just as delicious if you cook it right away.

In a grill pan, heat the canola oil over medium-high heat. Season the fish with salt. Grill the fillets, turning once, until browned on both sides and just opaque, 3 to 4 minutes per side.

Serve with salt and vinegar chips.

SHAWARMA

HARISSA MAYO/PICKLES

Makes 4 servings

Chicken shawarma is usually made on a rotating spit with marinated pieces of thigh and lamb fat, slowly roasting and crisping as it turns. I love the flavor of the spice combination. Keeping a jar of Shawarma Spice Mix (page 159) in your pantry can take you from boring grilled chicken to "Oh, snap! That's a tasty chicken" with no extra time. I don't know why you would ever make bland chicken ever again. You better not.

I almost always eat mayo with my chicken. Mayo girl here. To upgrade the mayo for my shawarma, I make a quick harissa mayo. Store-bought harissa can be great. Just be sure to taste it for its spice level before adding the quantity in the recipe. If you can't find Israeli pickles, try to find something that's brined in salt and not sweet at all, such as a kosher dill pickle.

THE THINGS

1½ cups (338 g) full-fat mayonnaise

1 to 3 tbsp (15 to 45 g) harissa (depending on spiciness)

4 boneless, skinless chicken breasts

¼ cup (30 g) Shawarma Spice Mix (page 159)

Kosher salt

Freshly ground black pepper

Canola oil, for frying

Fluffy pocket pita, seeded sliced bread, focaccia, naan or any other good bread you have

Sliced Israeli pickles

Sliced tomatoes

THE WAY

In a small bowl, mix together the mayo and harissa. Set in the fridge until ready to use.

Slice the breasts in half for thinner, quick-cooking pieces by placing the breast on a cutting board, and with your hand flat on top, slice into one side of the breast, slicing the entire way through. If the breasts are thick, try slicing them into three cutlets.

Season the cutlets generously with the shawarma spice, salt and pepper.

In a large skillet, heat about 1 tablespoon (15 ml) of the oil over medium-low heat. Cook the cutlets, in batches so as to not crowd the skillet, until golden brown, 3 to 4 minutes. Flip and continue to cook until cooked through, 2 to 3 more minutes. Repeat with the remaining cutlets.

Spread a generous amount of mayo onto both sides of the inside of the pita or bread. Fill the sandwich with lots of chicken shawarma, Israeli pickles and slices of tomato.

HOT TIPS

- For a more classic flavor, swap out the harissa mayo for some tahini sauce (page 102).

- If using sliced bread, give it a little toast.

- Make this shawarma and put it on some rice; call it a bowl.

- Literally do anything with this chicken that you are doing on a regular chicken basis.

VEGETABLES & RICE

THE WAY YOU CUT A VEGETABLE IS AS IMPORTANT AS CUTTING STEAK AGAINST THE GRAIN. You can have the same ingredients in the same salad, but have the flavor completely change depending on how it's cut. For example, take cucumbers, tomatoes and red onions. Chop into super-small pieces and have yourself a delicious Israeli salad with lots of salt and olive oil. Now, take those same vegetables and cut them into large, irregular shapes and call it a Greek salad. It will taste different because in one, you'll be able to get a few flavors in one bite, and in the second, you'll have moments of each vegetable that you're chewing more, tasting each component separately. How you cut that veg is so important. Keep that in mind the next time you're holding a butternut squash. Are you going to cut it into small cubes, large cubes, steaks, Hasselback, just in half, large irregular shapes . . . the possibilities are endless, really.

Rice can be a savior. It can be clean and just an accompaniment or a meal in itself. We almost always had rice with our dinner growing up. Maybe it was just an easy way to add another component, but I loved mixing it with the other flavors on my plate. Today, I find that I'm flavoring my rice as I would anything else: with spices, nuts, beans and herbs. The comfort of a bowl of rice can turn my day around. With such flavors as curry and baharat, the rice takes on life.

I'll say it again: Don't try to go crazy if you're just working on getting dinner on the table. Start thinking about how you can adjust your usual dishes to be a bit different and more thrilling. Cut that vegetable in a different way, add a quick tahini sauce (page 102), smash and tear that cucumber and get something new from your salads. Throw in some nuts or simply add some new spice or seed to that pot of rice. And, as with everything, when in doubt, put some chimichurri on it.

FRIED RICE

CURRY/COCONUT MILK

Makes 4 servings

This is going to be another one of those Dad recipes. Man, he loves curry powder (check out his Ravioli, page 47). He can literally make something from nothing. It's incredible to watch him work. He claps his hands and gets moving from the fridge, to the pantry, back to the fridge, then pulls out almost every spice in the cabinet and cooks you a meal bursting with bold flavors. The one thing he'd make on the regular was shakshuka and chicken curry.

This dish is hot, spiced, saucy and you can sit with it in front of the TV with a bowl and a spoon. Every curry powder is different. Mine is heavy on the turmeric and pretty mild, which is why I can use so much of it to get that punchy flavor. Using leftover rice from takeout is ideal here. I usually order extra when I'm getting Chinese delivered and then make this dish the next day, though I've totally made a pot of rice to make this. No shame there.

THE THINGS

2 tbsp (30 ml) canola oil

½ red onion, diced

4 cloves garlic, roughly chopped

3 to 4 tbsp (19 to 25 g) mild yellow curry powder

2 large eggs, lightly beaten

Kosher salt

2 cups (320 g) cooked long-grain rice

½ cup (120 ml) coconut milk

½ cup (65 g) frozen peas

Labne or Greek yogurt, for serving

Sriracha, for serving

THE WAY

In a large wok or nonstick skillet, heat the canola oil over medium-low heat. Add the red onion and garlic and cook until softened and fragrant, about 2 minutes. Stir in the curry powder and cook until fragrant, about 30 seconds. Push the onion and garlic toward the outer edge of the pan and add the beaten eggs to the center. Scramble until the eggs are mostly cooked. Season with a generous amount of salt. Add the rice and coconut milk and cook, mixing until it all comes together, about 1 minute. Add the frozen peas and cook until they are heated through, about 2 minutes. Taste and season with additional salt.

Divide among 4 serving bowls and top with labne and sriracha.

MASHED POTATOES

WHITE SWEET POTATOES/
BROWN BUTTER/VANILLA
BEAN/ALMONDS

Makes 6 servings

Batata sofrito: a dish of chicken and potatoes cooked in tons of oil and black pepper. I would mash the thick slices of potato and pour the "juice" from the pot onto it and call it mashed potatoes. That was the closest thing we got to traditional mashed potatoes growing up.

After cooking school, where we spent a full week on potatoes, I fell in love with the white sweet potato, which I use here. I find the flavor mildly sweet and this potato mashes very well. If you can't get your hands on white sweet potatoes, give it a shot with the orange- or even purple-fleshed potatoes. The brown butter with almonds and pine nuts will go with any of them. Give me all the sweet potato colors.

THE THINGS

Mashed Potatoes

1½ lb (680 g) white sweet potatoes, peeled and cut into 2" (5-cm) pieces

½ cup (120 ml) heavy cream

8 tbsp (112 g) unsalted butter, melted

1 tsp vanilla bean paste, or the beans scraped from 1 vanilla bean

Kosher salt

Browned Butter Topping

3 tbsp (21 g) slivered almonds

2 tbsp (18 g) pine nuts

4 tbsp (55 g) unsalted butter

6 large sage leaves

THE WAY

Place the potatoes in a large pot and cover with cold water. Bring to a boil, then lower the heat to medium-low and simmer until fork-tender, 10 to 12 minutes. Drain the potatoes. Pass them through the small-hole disk of a potato ricer, back into the pot they were cooked. Stir in the cream, melted butter, vanilla bean paste and salt to taste. Preheat the oven to 300°F (150°C).

Prepare the brown butter topping. On a dry baking sheet, toast the slivered almonds and pine nuts in the oven until lightly golden brown, 2 to 5 minutes. In a medium sauté pan, melt the butter over medium-high heat until it foams. Add the sage, almonds and pine nuts. Continue to cook, gently swirling the pan constantly, until the foam subsides and the butter is browned and nutty. *Immediately* pour over the plated mashed potatoes.

HOT TIPS

- You can hand mash the potatoes if you do not have a ricer.

- Gently warming the cream with the butter before mixing it into the potatoes will ensure you don't stir too much and make the potatoes gummy.

- Keep the mashed potatoes warm in a heatproof bowl, covered tightly with plastic wrap, *over* a pot of gently simmering water for up to an hour. If they get too thick, stir in a bit of cream.

- You can make the brown butter and set it aside in a bowl. Just don't leave it in the pan or else the butter will continue to cook and burn.

BROCCOLINI

SHAWARMA SPICE/TAHINI SAUCE/ LEMON

Makes 4 side servings

Roasted broccolini with tahini and lemon. I wrote this recipe and about a month later it showed up on my Instagram feed from *Bon Appétit*. I swear. Okay, it's not exactly the same, but it's freaking close.

Here's how my recipe differs: We have a shawarma moment here along with an awesome crunch mix. I make a big batch of Shawarma Spice Mix (page 159) in my pantry for times that I want a bit of punch added to chicken breast or any vegetable, really. This is a simple side dish that comes together quickly and can be served at room temperature, which makes it a perfect IMHO.

THE THINGS

2 bunches broccolini

3 tbsp (45 ml) olive oil

2 tsp (5 g) Shawarma Spice Mix (page 159)

Kosher salt

¼ cup (60 g) tahini

1 tbsp (15 ml) fresh lemon juice, plus more for serving

¼ to ⅓ cup (60 to 80 ml) cool water

1 tbsp (9 g) toasted pine nuts

1 tbsp (9 g) sunflower seeds

1 tsp toasted sesame seeds

Lemon wedges, to serve

THE WAY

Preheat the oven to 425°F (220°C). Cut the stems off the treelike tops and slice them ¼ inch (6 mm) thick. Transfer to a rimmed baking sheet, toss with the olive oil and shawarma spice and season with salt. Arrange the broccolini and the stems in a single layer. Roast for about 10 minutes, or until you have some nice, crisp edges.

Meanwhile, prepare the tahini sauce. In a small bowl, whisk together the tahini, lemon juice and a sprinkle of salt. Slowly pour in the water and whisk until you have a smooth sauce—you may need only ¼ cup (60 ml) of the water and you may need even more than ⅓ cup (80 ml). The finished product should be a sauce you can drizzle.

To finish, in a small bowl, combine the pine nuts, sunflower seeds and sesame seeds to make the crunch mix. Plate the broccolini, drizzle with the tahini sauce, top with the crunch mix and then squeeze some fresh lemon juice on top.

HOT TIPS

- The broccolini can easily be swapped out with reg' ol' broccoli.

- Try the same recipe but with butternut squash or acorn squash, carrots, cauliflower or any veg that you'd roast.

PANZANELLA

ZA'ATAR/OLIVES/MOZZARELLA/SUMAC SOURDOUGH

Makes 6 servings

I hate whole tomatoes. I especially hate little cherry tomatoes that pop in your mouth and fill it with sweet tomato juice. I know! I know! I'm the odd one out, for sure. That being said, I do love a good panzanella salad: a tomato and bread salad with a punchy vinaigrette. The only way I can actually stomach tomatoes is when they are accompanied by bread and vinegar, so this salad really works out. This salad lives on the border of Italian panzanella and Middle Eastern fattoush, which is really where I'd like to spend my summer days.

Making your own croutons is key here. Tearing the bread instead of cutting it creates irregular shapes that crisp up in the oven nicely. And if you're already tearing, go ahead and tear that mozz up, too, making it stringy and soft. You've got a beautiful balance of sweet tomatoes, creamy mozzarella, crispy, tangy croutons, herbaceous za'atar, salty olives and acidic vinegar. Perf salad.

THE THINGS

½ loaf sourdough bread, crust removed, torn into 1" (2.5-cm) pieces

3½ tbsp (53 ml) olive oil, divided

2 tsp (5 g) sumac

Kosher salt

1 lb (455 g) red and yellow cherry tomatoes, sliced in half

6 oz (170 g) fresh mozzarella cheese, torn into bite-size pieces

¼ cup (25 g) pitted and torn Italian green olives

¼ red onion, thinly sliced on a mandoline

2 tbsp (30 ml) white wine vinegar

1 tbsp (7 g) za'atar

Flaky sea salt

Fresh cilantro or other herb, for garnish

THE WAY

Prepare the croutons. Preheat the oven to 425°F (220°C). On a rimmed baking sheet, toss the torn bread, 1½ tablespoons (23 ml) of olive oil, sumac and salt to taste. Bake, tossing once halfway through, until golden brown, about 10 minutes.

In a large bowl, combine the tomatoes, mozzarella, olives, onion and croutons with the white wine vinegar, 2 tablespoons (30 ml) of olive oil, za'atar and flaky sea salt. Toss the salad gently with your hands until dressed. Plate and garnish with cilantro leaves or other herbs you have on hand.

HOT TIPS

- You can make the croutons ahead. Just allow them to cool completely before storing them in a resealable plastic bag for up to 2 days.

- If you are making the salad ahead of time, toss the ingredients together *without* the croutons, vinegar, olive oil, za'atar and sea salt. Only dress the salad and add the croutons right before you're ready to serve.

GREEN BEANS

SNOW PEAS/ZA'ATAR/
YOGURT

Makes 4 side servings

I hated blanching in culinary school. My chefs were extremely picky about the doneness of the vegetables, and therefore I had to make them over and over until I got it right. I avoid blanching like the plague in my kitchen. I will always find another way.

French green beans, for example, are excellent when they're blanched perfectly and tossed with a lemon vinaigrette. But my shortcut to great green beans is grilling. It's easy, quick and foolproof. A lot more forgiving than blanching, not to mention a hell of a lot tastier when you add that light char flavor. #maillardreaction

THE THINGS

1 lb (455 g) French green beans, trimmed

½ lb (225 g) snow peas

2 tbsp (30 ml) olive oil

2 tbsp (15 g) za'atar

Kosher salt

Freshly ground black pepper

1 cup (230 g) Greek yogurt

3 tbsp (45 ml) water

THE WAY

In a large bowl, toss together the green beans, snow peas, olive oil, za'atar and salt and pepper to taste.

Heat a grill pan or skillet over medium-high heat. In batches, add the beans to the skillet in a single layer. Cook, tossing occasionally, until lightly charred and tender, about 5 minutes. Continue until all the beans are grilled.

In a small bowl, thin out the Greek yogurt with some water (you may not need all of it) and season with lots of salt. Serve with the grilled beans.

SLAW

SUMAC/PEPITAS/
SUNFLOWER SEEDS/
BLUE CHEESE

Makes 4 to 6 servings

The mandoline is the most dangerous tool in the kitchen. On multiple occasions, I had to send employees home because they'd cut themselves so badly that they couldn't continue working that day. I sent the same guy home twice from the same type of mandoline injury, but in retrospect, he had other issues. Now, you can definitely slice up some cabbage really thinly and evenly with time and patience or mad knife skills, but I recommend using a mandoline for slaw. Just be super-careful, please.

This slaw is so much more than a regular tangle of cabbage. The pepitas and sunflower seeds add the perfect extra crunch and seedy flavor. But the real star here is the blue cheese. The funk and creaminess is such a good balance to the tart, acidic dressing.

THE THINGS

1 small head purple cabbage, finely shredded on a mandoline

2 Persian cucumbers, finely sliced on a mandoline

½ cup (70 g) roasted pepitas

¼ cup (36 g) roasted sunflower seeds

2½ to 3 tbsp (38 to 45 ml) fresh lemon juice

2 tbsp (30 ml) olive oil

1 tsp sumac

Kosher salt

¼ cup (30 g) Point Reyes blue cheese, crumbled

THE WAY

In a large bowl, toss together the cabbage, cucumbers, pepitas, sunflower seeds, lemon juice, olive oil, sumac and lots of kosher salt.

Top with the crumbled blue cheese and serve.

CAESAR

TAHINI/AVOCADO/SUMAC CROUTONS

Makes 4 servings

Kale Caesar has become a thing. I've seen it on almost each menu of every trendy new restaurant I've been to. We're all trying to upgrade the basic Caesar salad. But now that a kale Caesar is so mainstream, giving it a new little twist is all it needs to be exciting again. Tahini: the answer to all my questions.

Tahini adds a nuttiness to Caesar dressing that you wouldn't be able to get unless you've added pine nuts to it. But you won't say, "Oh wow, that tastes like you added tahini to Caesar dressing." It will be subtle and easy to fall in love with. In a salad like this, where there aren't a ton of components, I feel it necessary to put a bit more effort into making croutons from scratch. It really isn't hard or time consuming. The addition of sumac to the crispy croutons gives them a little sour punch to counterbalance the creamy avocado. And Parm, of course.

THE THINGS

3 thick slices sourdough bread, torn into 1" (2.5-cm) pieces

3½ tbsp (53 ml) olive oil

2 tsp (5 g) sumac

Kosher salt

3 tbsp (45 g) tahini

2 cloves garlic, grated on a microplane

1½ tbsp (23 ml) fresh lemon juice

¼ cup (25 g) grated Parmesan cheese, plus more for serving

1 tsp Dijon mustard

3 to 4 tbsp (45 to 60 ml) water

Freshly ground black pepper

8 cups (536 g) chopped lacinato kale

1 tsp fresh lemon juice

1 avocado, peeled, pitted and sliced, for serving

THE WAY

Prepare the croutons. Preheat the oven (or a toaster oven) to 400°F (200°C). In a bowl, toss the sourdough with the olive oil, sumac and lots of salt. Spread on a rimmed baking sheet and bake, tossing once halfway through, until golden brown and crisp, 10 to 12 minutes.

Prepare the dressing. In a small bowl, whisk together the tahini, garlic, lemon juice, Parmesan, Dijon, water, salt and pepper. If the consistency is too thick, add a bit more water.

Prepare the salad. Toss the kale, lemon juice and a few good pinches of salt in a salad bowl. Using your hands, massage the kale until it just starts to wilt. Don't overdo it or else it'll become rubbery and limp. Add the croutons and a few tablespoons of the dressing and toss with your hands. Divide the salad among 4 bowls and top with sliced avocado and shaved Parmesan. Serve with extra dressing on the side.

CELERY

WHITE PEPPER/GOAT
CHEESE/HAZELNUTS

Makes 4 servings

The most underrated vegetable: celery. It's a workhorse in almost every single soup and stock and lasts forever in the fridge. You can regrow it from a stump and use every part of it from the leaves to the roots. The humble garnish to your Bloody Mary, the cute kids' snack filled with peanut butter (yeah, that's weird). Best yet, it burns more calories to chew and digest than it actually has in it. Don't bypass it. Don't wave it off as a garbage vegetable.

When you slice celery on the diagonal, you can eat it raw without being bothered by those stringy bits. I love ground white pepper more than its brother, black pepper, for its acidic quality. Just a tiny bit of it goes a long way. The goat cheese adds a needed fattiness that cuts the harsh red wine vinegar. Another thing to love about this salad is that it doesn't really go limp, even hours after you've dressed it, so it's great for dinner parties. It can sit on the table the entire time and doesn't lose its oomph.

THE THINGS

6 to 8 celery ribs, thinly sliced on a diagonal

2 tbsp (8 g) celery leaves

¼ cup (29 g) roughly chopped, roasted hazelnuts

2½ tbsp (38 ml) good-quality olive oil

2 tbsp (30 ml) red wine vinegar

½ tsp honey

Kosher salt

2 pinches of ground white pepper

¼ cup (68 g) crumbled goat cheese

THE WAY

In a large bowl, toss together the celery, celery leaves, roasted hazelnuts, olive oil, red wine vinegar, honey, salt and white pepper.

Top with the crumbled goat cheese.

HOT TIPS

- You can slice the celery on a mandoline for perfection.

- Add golden raisins for sweetness.

- Toast some cumin or caraway seeds, then crush and add to the mixture.

- Add some very thinly sliced fennel.

WHITE RICE

CUCUMBERS/CASHEWS/
CILANTRO/MINT

Makes 4 servings

For this recipe, you'll need to cook the rice using the "lots of water" method, which basically translates to "you're going to cook the rice like pasta." This is the easiest method to get perfectly cooked rice that is not overcooked and bursting, or undercooked and still crunchy. It's the best way to cook rice if you're looking for it to have that single grain-by-grain thing happen. Exactly what you would want for this type of "rice salad." Lime juice and a tiny bit of Asian fish sauce really brighten up the herby rice. Cashews take it from a 6 to a 9.8, though. It hits the palate in almost all the ways. Perfect to serve in the spring or summer as a side dish.

THE THINGS

½ cup (98 g) uncooked basmati or jasmine rice

2 tbsp (30 ml) fresh lime juice

1 tbsp (15 ml) sesame oil

1½ tsp (10 g) agave nectar or honey

½ tsp Asian fish sauce

Kosher salt

1 Persian cucumber, thinly sliced

½ cup (70 g) whole roasted cashews

2 tbsp (6 g) finely chopped fresh chives

1½ tbsp (4 g) finely chopped fresh cilantro

1 tbsp (6 g) fine ribbons of or finely chopped fresh mint

THE WAY

Bring a large pot of salted water to a boil over high heat. Add the rice and cook like pasta until cooked through, 8 to 10 minutes. You can taste as it cooks, which is the beauty of this cooking method. Drain into a fine-mesh sieve and rinse with cold water.

In a small bowl, whisk together the lime juice, sesame oil, agave, fish sauce and a pinch or two of salt.

In a bowl, combine the rice, cucumber, cashews, chives, cilantro, mint and dressing. Serve at room temp or cold.

HOT TIPS

· Use brown rice, wild rice, barley, farro or another grain instead.

· Swap out the cashews for pine nuts or peanuts for a different crunch.

· Add shredded chicken and a drizzle of tahini sauce (page 102).

· Okay, secret: I don't rinse rice. I'm too lazy. Things come out pretty well regardless.

RICE & BEANS

BAHARAT/BLACK BEANS/
OLIVES/BANANAS

Makes 4 servings

Growing up, we had Cuban family friends that we became very close with. We would eat over at one another's houses, go on vacations and celebrate holidays together. My friend Jenny and I watched Baz Luhrmann's *Romeo + Juliet* a million times while her mom would be downstairs cooking *picadillo*, a Cuban dish made with ground beef, spices and olives. They would serve this with rice and beans and sliced bananas. Yes, sliced bananas. It's a Cuban thing, and it's insanely delicious. The combination of salty and sweet just works so well.

This is my ode to my adopted Cuban roots. It's just a humble rice dish made with warming and savory baharat spice mix (page 159), black beans and some of the things you'd find in picadillo, such as olives and bananas. It's a simple side that has a lot going on and can hold its own. Cooking the rice with the olives brings a gentle acidity that brightens an otherwise one-note ingredient in rice. This would be perfect with the steak from page 71.

THE THINGS

1½ tbsp (23 ml) olive oil

2 cloves garlic, roughly chopped

2 tsp (5 g) Baharat Mix (page 159)

1 cup (195 g) uncooked long-grain white rice

1 (15-oz [425-g]) can black beans, drained and rinsed

½ cup (50 g) whole manzanilla olives with pimientos, 2 tbsp (30 ml) brine reserved

2 cups (475 ml) water

Kosher salt

Freshly ground black pepper

Chopped fresh cilantro, for garnish

Slices of banana, for serving

THE WAY

In a large saucepan, heat the olive oil over medium heat. Add the garlic and baharat and cook until fragrant, about 30 seconds. Add the rice and cook, stirring occasionally, until the rice is slightly translucent, about 2 minutes. Add the black beans, olives, reserved olive brine and water and season with lots of salt and pepper. Increase the heat to high and bring to a boil. Lower the heat, cover and simmer until the rice is tender and has absorbed all the water, 15 to 18 minutes. Turn off the heat and *do not lift the lid*. Allow the rice to steam for an additional 10 minutes.

Fluff the rice and garnish with chopped cilantro. Serve with sliced bananas.

TOAST

There is a right way and a wrong way to make toast. I believe that sticking a slice of bread in one of those pop-up-when-it's-ready toasters is so 1900s. The bread has to be a specific size for these machines and the slices almost always pop out dry and either over- or under-toasted. Not my favorite. Keep those around for Pop-Tarts and to reheat McDonald's hash browns. When I say "toast," I'm talking about an open-faced sandwich that is hefty enough to eat as a meal, like a real hipster. It can be eaten with a knife and fork or by hand. It has components, but keep things simple by concentrating on only one element of the toast and keeping the rest pretty raw. It can be filling, comforting and satisfying or just a really awesome snack.

A great toast doesn't need to start from fresh bread. *Always* keep sliced bread in the freezer. When I go out to the bakery or farmers' market (or even Costco), I pick out a fresh, crusty loaf of bread. As soon as I can, I slice it, place it neatly and tightly in a resealable plastic bag and throw it right into the freezer. If I know I'm having some that day, I will keep that section, unsliced, covered on the counter. But literally everything else goes into the freezer. It can stay "fresh" like that for more than a month. When I'm ready, I take a slice and microwave it for 25 to 30 seconds, wrapped in a damp paper towel. Fresher than the day I bought it. Seriously. I've got olive bread from the neighborhood bakery, sourdough from the farmers' market, seedy grainy bread from Costco (it's really, really good), a carrot spelt loaf from the Mexican bakery across town, pitas from the kosher shop up the street and bagels from New Jersey. My freezer is filled with more bread products than anything else.*

I like to slice my bread a bit thicker than the standard; ¾ to 1 inch (2 to 2.5 cm) thick. It feels heartier and holds up to toppings a lot better. I would also like to admit at this moment that I have an addiction to bread, so . . . a 1-inch (2.5-cm) slice is real nice. A thick slice of bread that is crispy and golden brown and still a bit squishy and soft at the same time is ideal for toast making. This can be achieved in multiple ways. In all methods, the beginnings are the same.

*Correction: I have **a lot** of chicken nuggets and cookie dough balls in my freezer, too.

CLASSIC TOAST

OLIVE OIL/SEA SALT

Makes 1 serving

A good piece of toast starts with good bread. You want something that has a nice crust and a soft, spongey interior. I love everything from a sourdough to a dark, dense pumpernickel. Be sure that the bread you toast complements what you're going to load it up with! And don't forget, lots of good olive oil is key.

THE THINGS

High-quality bread, sliced yourself to 1" (2.5 cm) thick

High-quality olive oil

Flaky sea salt

Freshly ground black pepper

THE WAY

Generously drizzle the slices with olive oil (only on one side, unless noted by the cooking method) and press it into the nooks and crannies with your fingers. Sprinkle with flaky sea salt and freshly ground black pepper. Now, you'll want heat:

Pan-grilled: Heat a grill pan or cast-iron pan over medium-high heat. Grill the bread until golden brown, 1½ to 2 minutes on the first side and 30 seconds to 1 minute on the second side. (For this method, drizzle oil on both sides of the sliced bread.)

Toaster oven-ed: Toast on HIGH for 3 minutes with the rack set in the middle of the toaster oven.

Broiled: Set the oven rack to the top third and preheat the broiler to high. Place the oiled slices of bread on a baking sheet and broil until golden brown, about 1½ minutes. Every oven is different and you'll want to keep your eye on these *the entire time* until you feel they're ready.

Grilled: For this method, drizzle oil on both sides of the sliced bread. Heat a grill over high, direct heat. Grill the bread until golden brown, 1½ to 2 minutes on the first side and 30 seconds to 1 minute on the second side, leaving the lid of the grill open.

Campfire: For this method, drizzle oil on both sides of the sliced bread. Stick the sliced bread on a poker and place it inches from the fire while rotating constantly until golden brown, 1 to 2 minutes.

AVOCADO TOAST

CHIMICHURRI/PROSCIUTTO

Makes 1 serving with extra chimichurri

Okay, okay. Avocado toast has had its moment. But I'm not over it and I know you're not, either. It's the most basic of things that are the most satisfying in the end. I don't care how hipster or millennial it is, crispy, toasted bread topped with a heap of creamy avocado, with a squeeze of citrus and a sprinkle of salt and white pepper, is just heaven on Earth. There are a billion different kinds of versions out there. I'm sure you have your own little twist or favorite way to have avocado toast, but this is my upgraded version.

Chimichurri. The ultimate sauce, dressing, seasoning, dip, however you use it. It works well on everything from steak to eggs or from tofu to acorn squash. It brightens up any heavy dish and adds a punch to the most delicate of vegetables. Hands down, it's my favorite sauce (other than tahini, of course). On this toast, you got a crusty bread, smooth avocado, salty prosciutto and acidic chimichurri. It's both beautifully showstopping and delicious.

THE THINGS

¼ cup (60 ml) good-quality olive oil

1 clove garlic, grated on a microplane

1 to 2 scallions, finely sliced

1 tbsp (3 g) finely chopped fresh cilantro

1 tbsp (15 ml) fresh lime juice

1 tbsp (15 ml) red wine vinegar

¼ tsp Aleppo pepper flakes, Urfa or basic crushed red pepper flakes

Pinch of paprika

Pinch of dried oregano

Kosher salt

1 slice sourdough bread, toasted (recommended method: broiled)

½ ripe avocado, peeled, pitted and sliced or mashed

4 slices good-quality prosciutto

Freshly ground black pepper

THE WAY

Prepare the chimichurri. In a bowl, combine the olive oil, garlic, scallions, cilantro, lime juice, red wine vinegar, Aleppo pepper, paprika, oregano and salt to taste, then set aside.

Top the sourdough toast with nicely sliced or mashed avocado. Beautifully heap the slices of prosciutto onto the avocado in a way that gives the prosciutto volume and body. Drizzle with lots and lots of chimichurri and season with black pepper.

HOT TIPS

- If you're serving this for brunch, you can add some six-minute eggs (page 129) on top, too. Or if you have a precision cooker, a sous vide egg would be so perfect.

- Swap out prosciutto for hard salami.

- This is a perfect buffet brunch dish; lay out all the ingredients and have your guests make their own toast. Less work for you.

- Serve this chimichurri over *everything*.

BEAN TOAST

REFRIED BEANS/EGG

Makes 2 servings

Mexican leftovers become incredible breakfast beginnings. Just simply heating them up in a pan and throwing a fried egg on top will make you the most effortless breakfast you didn't have to cook. We've been known to over-order on purpose to make sure there is enough for the next morning. My favorite part of Mexican leftovers for breakfast is the refried beans. Normally overlooked as the thing that comes alongside the food you ordered, it's the perfect breakfast beginnings. When I don't have leftover refried beans but still want some, I make these quick, spiced beans that really hit the spot.

This bean recipe can be made the night before if you don't have much time in the morning. Usually refried beans are made with pinto beans, but I had great northern beans in my pantry and went with those. Be fluid with this recipe and just use what you have on hand. Talk about an excellent pantry meal! Try this with chickpeas instead of great northern beans!

THE THINGS

2 tbsp (30 ml) olive oil

1 clove garlic, grated on a microplane

½ tsp paprika

½ tsp dried oregano

¼ tsp ground coriander

¼ tsp ground cumin

1 (15.5-oz [440-g]) can great northern beans, drained and rinsed

Kosher salt

2 slices 100% dark rye or pumpernickel bread, toasted (recommended method: pan-grilled)

2 fried eggs (page 30, minus the curry powder)

Flaky sea salt, for garnish

Fresh cilantro leaves, for garnish

THE WAY

In a skillet, heat the olive oil over medium heat. Add the garlic and cook until just fragrant, about 30 seconds. Add the paprika, oregano, coriander and cumin and cook until the oils have developed, about another 30 seconds. Add the beans and toss to coat. Season with kosher salt and cook until the beans are warmed through, about 2 minutes.

Top the toast with a generous portion of beans and lay a fried egg on top. Garnish with flaky sea salt and cilantro leaves.

CUCUMBER TOAST

LABNE/RADISH/ALEPPO/DILL

Makes 2 servings

The cucumber sandwich: traditionally made with thin slices of cucumber on crustless white bread. The British really know how to get you excited for a sandwich. I've seen them hanging out at banquet hall–type events with cream cheese and dill; nonetheless, they are just so freaking bland. That being said, I can never resist one. Maybe it will be tasty? It never is.

This is what I would like a cucumber sandwich to taste like: lightly toasted rye bread, a good smear of labne and topped with dressed and well-salted cucumbers. Crispy, salty, lemony, creamy, crunchy, a bit spicy, it hits the palate in all the right places.

THE THINGS

2 Persian cucumbers, thinly sliced lengthwise on a mandoline

2 to 3 radishes, thinly sliced on a mandoline

1 tbsp (4 g) finely chopped fresh dill

1 tbsp (15 ml) fresh lemon juice

1½ tsp (30 ml) good-quality olive oil

½ tsp Aleppo pepper flakes

Flaky sea salt

2 slices thin rye bread, toasted (recommended method: toaster oven-ed lightly)

Labne

THE WAY

In a bowl, toss the cucumbers and radishes with the dill, lemon juice, olive oil, Aleppo and a healthy pinch of flaky sea salt.

Top the toast with a healthy layer of labne. Arrange the cucumbers and radishes on the labne.

HOT TIPS

- Hear me out: Sprinkle a tiny pinch of MSG on the cucumbers and radishes when you toss them. The flavor changes and becomes super-savory. Don't hate MSG; it's just umami salt.

- Replace the Aleppo with red pepper flakes in a pinch.

- Add some sprouts or arugula and make a cucumber sandwich.

EGG TOAST

SIX-MINUTE EGG/BEET
HORSERADISH MAYO/
RADISH

Makes 4 servings

There used to be a strip mall restaurant in Atlanta called Bagel Palace, an institution really, that served breakfast and Jewish deli favorites. It was extremely saddening to hear it was closing its doors after 25 years in business because the rent was too high. My husband and I were there every weekend, getting a toasted pumpernickel bagel with egg salad piled high and a side of pasta salad. It was the closest thing to a New York–style bagel I could get down here in the South

Here, instead of chopping the eggs and mixing them with mayo, I decided it would be more exciting as a deconstructed toast than a sandwich. The mayo has a Jewish deli vibe with the beet horseradish mixed in. I love Kewpie mayo because it feels hefty and super-eggy. This is an ode to my Bagel Palace egg salad sandwich.

THE THINGS

1½ tsp (8 g) spicy beet horseradish

½ cup (115 g) Kewpie brand mayonnaise

4 large eggs

4 thick slices rye or pumpernickel, toasted (recommended method: pan-grilled)

1 medium watermelon radish, thinly sliced on a mandoline

Thinly sliced fresh chives

Flaky sea salt

Freshly ground black pepper

THE WAY

Prepare the beet horseradish mayo. In a small bowl, stir the beet horseradish and mayo.

Prepare the eggs. Bring a pot of water to a rapid boil and prepare an ice bath in a large bowl. Gently lower each egg into the boiling water and boil for exactly 6½ minutes. Immediately transfer the eggs to the ice bath. Allow to cool for 2 minutes. Peel.

Spread the beet horseradish mayo on the toasted rye. Place 3 to 4 slices of radish on each toast. Lay an egg on top and gently smash it open with a fork. You can also tear it into large pieces, taking care that the jammy yolk runs onto the toast. Garnish with chives, flaky sea salt and pepper.

HOT TIPS

- Can't find Kewpie mayo? Just use what you have. Or dare to make your own aioli?

- Can't get your hands on a watermelon radish? Regular radishes are good, too.

- Use kitchen shears to cut the chives.

- Use this beet mayo on any sandwich!

- If you hate peeling eggs, you can make a fried egg instead (page 30, minus the curry powder).

TUNA TOAST

AVOCADO/SESAME OIL/
SCALLIONS

Makes 2 servings

How do you feel about having tuna salad for breakfast? It's been an ongoing debate with the people in my life. I grew up having tuna on a bagel for breakfast. It makes a lot of sense in my head, but after bringing some to work one morning a few years back, I was shocked to find out that this is not a thing. Or is it a thing and they're wrong? So, cream cheese and lox is cool for your first meal of the day, but tuna salad is a no-go? Come on. It's also perfect for when you're on that slow-carb diet and you're told to eat 30 grams of protein within 30 minutes of waking up. That's like forcing five eggs down. I prefer having a can of tuna, thanks.

Who are those select few who don't like mayo? We're not friends. I've got a lot of questions. But, anyway, this is the recipe for you. The avocado here doesn't only please the millennials, but also adds a flavorful fat instead of mayo. The creaminess is unbeatable. The addition of scallions and sesame oil gives it more of an Asian vibe. Like.

THE THINGS

1 ripe avocado, peeled and pitted

1 (5-oz [140-g]) can tuna in water, drained

3 to 4 scallions, finely sliced

1½ tbsp (4 g) finely chopped fresh cilantro

2 tbsp (30 ml) fresh lime juice

1 tbsp (15 ml) sesame oil

Kosher salt

2 thick slices country bread, toasted (recommended method: toaster oven-ed)

Black sesame seeds, for garnish

Flaky sea salt, for garnish

Sliced scallions, for garnish

THE WAY

Prepare the tuna salad. In a bowl, smash the avocado with a fork until very coarsely mashed. Add the drained tuna and mix until it's combined and the tuna has broken apart. Mix in the scallions, cilantro, lime juice, sesame oil and kosher salt to taste.

Top each toast with the tuna salad. Garnish with black sesame seeds, flaky sea salt and more scallions.

HOT TIPS

- The tuna salad will keep in the fridge for a day or two in a sealed container.

- Ummm . . . tuna melt, anyone? Top the tuna toast with sliced tomatoes and Swiss cheese, then stick under the broiler and broil until bubbly and hot.

- Make some sushi rice and top it with the tuna and you've got a "Low-Rent" Tuna Poke Bowl.

TOAST CON TOMATE

GRATED TOMATO/VINEGAR/
OLIVE BREAD

Makes 4 servings

When my husband and I took our honeymoon, three years after marriage, we fell in love with a small tapas spot in Barcelona. You had to walk down a flight of stairs to get to it. It sat maybe 20 people. For the life of me, I cannot remember what it was called or whether it even had a name. Like real idiots, we never wrote it down. This is where we had *pan con tomate* until we physically could not eat anymore.

I hate biting into a tomato almost as much as I hate taking a bite out of fruit. Unless it's peak tomato season, I don't find them appealing. Grated tomatoes pop up in a lot of Middle Eastern cooking. They're almost always served with Israeli breakfasts. I can do grated tomatoes. Must just be a texture thing I have going on. (For example, I will not eat oysters.)

THE THINGS

4 to 5 Roma tomatoes, halved through stem spot

1 clove garlic, grated on a microplane

1 tsp white wine vinegar

2 tbsp (30 ml) good-quality olive oil, plus more for drizzling

Kosher salt

4 slices black olive bread, toasted (recommended method: toaster oven-ed)

Flaky sea salt, for sprinkling

THE WAY

Using the large holes on a box grater set inside a bowl, grate the cut side of the tomatoes until you're left with the skin. Add the garlic, white wine vinegar, olive oil and kosher salt and mix.

Top the toasted black olive bread with a few tablespoons of the tomato mixture, drizzle with a bit of olive oil and season with flaky sea salt.

HOT TIPS

- Add a bit of harissa for heat.

- Use this as a sauce for roasted vegetables with tahini.

- This can also be served as a dipping sauce alongside a plate of oil and vinegar with good bread, for a nice appetizer.

LIVER TOAST

BALSAMIC/LUXARDO CHERRIES

Makes 2 servings

I never drank while growing up because I simply did not like the taste of alcohol. Until my developed palate discovered bourbon. When I order one at dinner, I always make sure they give me those beautiful deep burgundy orbs of the gods, a.k.a. Luxardo cherries. They taste of amaretto and an Italian coast. The OG of maraschino cherries. Not those neon red things you get at The Cheesecake Factory. The syrup they come in is just as valuable as the cherries themselves. I know they are expensive, but you are an adult and you're allowed to treat yourself.

The balance here of the savory livers with the acidic balsamic and the sweet cherries is perfection. This toast is like candy.

THE THINGS

½ lb (225 g) chicken livers

1 tbsp (15 ml) olive oil

2 tbsp (28 g) unsalted butter

Kosher salt

2 tbsp (30 ml) balsamic vinegar

2 slices country bread, toasted (recommended method: toaster oven-ed or broiled)

8 to 10 Luxardo cherries, plus their syrup

Flaky sea salt

Freshly ground black pepper

THE WAY

Rinse the livers and pat dry. Using a sharp knife, remove as much of the connective tissue as possible.

In a large skillet, heat the oil and butter over medium heat. Season the livers with kosher salt. Once the butter begins to bubble, add the livers. Cook, undisturbed, until browned but still pink in the middle, flipping them once halfway through cooking, 1 to 2 minutes per side. Deglaze the pan with the balsamic vinegar and cook until the vinegar reduces slightly, about 1 minute.

Divide the livers between the toasted bread slices and top with 4 or 5 cherries per toast. Drizzle some of the syrup onto the livers and season generously with flaky sea salt and pepper.

HOT TIPS

- Watch your face. Liver pops when it cooks and you have to be careful not to get hit with a ball of fiery oil from hell.

- You can order Luxardo cherries from Amazon. Yes, they're expensive. Yes, they are worth it. Yes, you will eat them straight out of the jar at 11:00 p.m., but only one . . . okay, two.

TAHINI TOAST

BANANA/SILAN/
PISTACHIOS/CHOCOLATE
SPRINKLES

Makes as many as you need

As much as I love a savory tahini, a sweet tahini is a thousand times better. I've been known to fill a bowl with 50 percent yogurt and 45 percent tahini. The remaining 5 percent is normally chocolate sprinkles.

This is what I make when I need a sweet breakfast on the fly; no time for pancakes, waffles or French toast. Tahini and silan, a date syrup, go together like sweatpants and a rainy day. One is nutty and sticky and the other is sweet and smooth. It lasts forever in your pantry and can be used in almost any recipe that calls for honey. Yes, sprinkles on toast. The Dutch do it, so don't @ me. There are no quantities to this recipe because you can use as much or as little of each ingredient as you'd like.

THE THINGS

Tahini

Slices of country bread or sourdough, toasted (recommended method: toaster oven-ed *without pepper*)

Sliced banana

Silan (date syrup)

Pistachios

Dark chocolate sprinkles

Flaky sea salt

THE WAY

Spread a generous amount of tahini on the toasted bread. Top with sliced banana, a drizzle of silan, pistachios, chocolate sprinkles and a bit of flaky sea salt.

HOT TIPS

- My favorite chocolate sprinkles come from a Dutch company called De Ruijter. Seriously, number one sprinkles in the world. You can find some on Amazon.

- Use almonds or any other nuts you have on hand if you don't usually have pistachios at home.

- If you don't have silan, you can definitely use honey.

CHOCOLATE TOAST

GELATO/OLIVE OIL/ITALIAN ROLL

Makes as many as you like

The same tapas spot in Barcelona where we had the pan con tomate (page 133) served a simple scoop of super-dark chocolate mousse with a light drizzle of olive oil, salt and crostini. This is the perfect balance of savory and sweet. I've taken those basic flavors and turned them into an easy store-bought dessert that takes almost no effort. It's a great conversation starter, too. People will be shocked when you start spreading softened chocolate ice cream on toasted bread.

THE THINGS

Squishy Italian sub rolls, sliced open

Good-quality dark chocolate gelato, softened but not melted

Good-quality olive oil

Flaky sea salt

THE WAY

When toasting the roll (recommended: the broiler method, page 121), use lots of olive oil and salt, but you can choose either to use black pepper or not. It works both ways.

Let the toast cool slightly and then spread a generous layer of ice cream on the cut side. Drizzle with olive oil and season with flaky sea salt. Serve immediately.

HOT TIPS

- Make sure you're using a high-quality dark chocolate gelato or super-creamy ice cream. This makes or breaks the toast. Talenti brand gelato is my favorite.

- Another key to this dish is to find that sweet spot of softened but not melted gelato.

- When it comes to the quality of your olive oil, break out the good stuff here.

DESSERTS

I've been known to make elaborate, 32-step, super-sugary desserts. Mostly because I enjoy it, but also because I had this idea that in order for dessert to impress, you had to take three days to make just one pie. I also had the luxury of taking my time. Now, I barely feel that I have time to get dinner ready, let alone think about making some crazy layer cake with Swiss meringue buttercream, crumbles, homemade jam to flavor the buttercream, a cake soak and tempered chocolate decorations.

These recipes are either quick to throw together or take very little active time. I wanted to be able to get one into the oven or fridge in a short amount of time, but also come out with something impressive with a unique taste.

SOME NOTES ON DESSERTS

- Get yourself a kitchen scale, please. It's more exact and also there's less cleanup.

- If a recipe doesn't specify which size eggs, always use large ones.

- Vanilla bean paste is a miracle substance.

- You have to use good-quality chocolate; otherwise, what's the point?

- More important, get yourself some good, unsweetened cocoa powder. I like Cocoa Barry's and Valrhona powders the best.

- Procrastibaking is a real thing. The Blondie recipe (page 142) is a good one for it.

BLONDIE

TAHINI/SESAME/
CHOCOLATE CHUNKS

*Makes one 9-inch (23-cm)
square pan*

I have been forbidden from making blondies at home because I will take down an entire pan before they're even cool enough to cut. I like blondies more than any brownie on earth and it's probably due to the fact that I love chocolate chip cookie dough so much.

Think of tahini as a peanut butter. It can be made sweet or salty or both. This bar is super-doughy and nutty with lots of chocolate and flaky sea salt. The more I make it, the more I fall in love with it. The great thing about it is that I can bring it to my daughter's school, because it is technically peanut-free.

THE THINGS

Cooking spray

8 tbsp (112 g) unsalted butter, melted

1 cup + 2 tbsp (225 g) granulated sugar

½ cup minus 2 tsp (105 g) light brown sugar

3 large eggs

1 cup (230 g) tahini

1½ tsp (8 g) vanilla bean paste

1⅔ cups (210 g) all-purpose flour

1 tsp kosher salt

1 cup (155 g) bittersweet chocolate chunks

Black and white sesame seeds

Flaky sea salt

THE WAY

Preheat the oven to 325°F (170°C). Grease a 9-inch (23-cm; 8-inch [20.5-cm] is fine, too) baking pan with cooking spray and line with parchment, leaving at least 2 inches (5 cm) of overhang on two opposite sides for easy removal.

In a large bowl, whisk together the melted butter, granulated sugar, brown sugar, eggs, tahini and vanilla bean paste until just combined. Add the flour and salt and fold in, using a rubber spatula, until just combined. Add the chocolate and fold again. Transfer the batter to the prepared pan. Garnish with lots of sesame seeds and flaky sea salt.

Bake in the middle of the oven for 24 to 28 minutes, or until the edges are golden brown and the middle is just beginning to set. Remove from the oven and allow to cool to room temperature in the pan before cutting into squares.

For perfectly cut bars, allow to cool in the fridge before cutting.

HOT TIPS

- Wrap it tightly and freeze half of the bar so you don't eat it all. Defrost in the fridge.

- Leave out the chocolate and add nuts.

- Warm it up and serve with ice cream and silan (date syrup).

CRISP

PLUM/GINGERSNAPS/
DRIED CHERRIES/WHIP

Makes 6 to 8 servings

I don't like fruit. This fruit dessert isn't about the fruit. The fruit here just adds a sweetness and juiciness to the crispy bits. But the real star here is the crumbly goodness that I layer underneath and on top of the fruit. If I could achieve that soft, doughy, sweet crumb that's wet and crispy at the same time without using fruit, I would. But unfortunately, it cannot be done. As it bakes, the juices from the plums drop to the bottom, giving you so much of that wet crumb, but leaving that top layer super-crisp.

I am in love with Anna's Ginger Swedish Thins. They're flower-shaped ginger cookies that are super-thin and crispy. They have the perfect blend of spices and I use them to make almost all my crumbles. They're amazing for icebox cake, too. If you can't seem to find them, any other gingersnap cookie will do! I always add salt to my baking, but because I am using salted butter here, there really is no need for extra.

THE THINGS

2 lb (905 g) black plums, sliced ⅓" (8 mm) thick

¼ cup (30 g) dried tart cherries (optional)

5 tbsp (38 g) all-purpose flour, divided

4 tbsp (60 g) light brown sugar, divided

1 (5.25-oz [150-g]) package Anna's Ginger Swedish Thins

½ cup (40 g) rolled oats

¼ cup (32 g) slivered almonds

7 tbsp (98 g) salted butter, melted

1½ cups (355 ml) heavy cream, optional

2 tbsp (26 g) granulated sugar, optional

Ground cinnamon, for sprinkling

THE WAY

Preheat the oven to 375°F (190°C) with the rack in the middle position. Butter a 7 x 11–inch (18 x 28–cm) baking dish or 8-inch (20.5-cm) square pan.

Prepare the plum mixture. In a large bowl, toss together the plums, dried cherries, 2 tablespoons (15 g) of flour and 2 tablespoons (30 g) of brown sugar, then set aside.

Prepare the crumb mixture. Break up the gingersnaps into pea-size pieces with either your hands, a food processor or a resealable plastic bag and a rolling pin . . . whatever works. In a large bowl, combine the ginger crumbs, 3 tablespoons (23 g) of flour, rolled oats, almonds, 2 tablespoons (30 g) of brown sugar and melted butter. Massage the melted butter into the crumb mixture and press it together with your hands to form clumps.

Press half of the crumb mixture into the bottom of the prepared baking dish and transfer the plums and all their accumulated juices on top. Compressing them in your fist to form clumps, scatter the remaining crumbs on top of the plums.

Bake until golden brown and juices are bubbling, 30 to 35 minutes.

Prepare the optional whip, but really, who would leave it out. In a large bowl, whisk the heavy cream and sugar until soft to medium peaks form.

Serve the crisp with the whip (if using) and a pinch of cinnamon.

MOUSSE

TAHINI/PISTACHIOS/
CHOCOLATE SPRINKLES

Makes 4 servings

After writing my first cookbook, *Modern Israeli Cooking*, I was invited to host a cookbook dinner at a restaurant in Atlanta called the General Muir. It was a super-success. Naturally, there was a lot of food. Guests enjoyed a six-course meal that featured some of my favorite recipes from the book, such as hummus, fattoush, Moroccan fish and braised pomegranate short ribs over peppery farrotto. I served a tahini mousse pie, which was not in the book, for dessert. Everyone, including the staff, let out an audible moan when tasting it. This mousse recipe was inspired by that pie.

If you've ever had peanut butter mousse and liked it, this is the recipe for you. Hip, Hip, Hooooo no-bake desserts for the win. This can hold up in the fridge for two days.

It's nice to let your guests build their own mousses with the various toppings. It's also less work for you. Silan (date syrup) is key, though, so please order some from Amazon.

THE THINGS

2¼ cups (535 ml) heavy cream, divided

½ tsp cream of tartar

⅔ cup (160 g) tahini

1½ cups (185 g) powdered sugar

1½ tsp (8 g) vanilla bean paste

Pinch of kosher salt

To Serve

Silan (date syrup)

Chopped pistachios

Dark chocolate sprinkles

Chocolate-covered quinoa (optional)

Flaky sea salt

THE WAY

In the bowl of an electric mixer fitted with the whisk attachment, combine 2 cups (475 ml) of the cream and the cream of tartar. Whisk the cream on medium speed at first and then on high speed until medium peaks form. Transfer to a different bowl and set aside.

Change to a paddle attachment (no need to clean the bowl). Mixing on low speed, combine the tahini, powdered sugar, vanilla bean paste and kosher salt until they just come together, about 30 seconds. While the mixer is running, very slowly drizzle in the remaining ¼ cup (60 ml) of cream. As soon as it's combined, turn off the mixer.

By hand, fold one-third of the whipped cream mixture into the tahini mixture. Be a bit aggressive with this first addition. Once almost combined, add another one-third of whipped cream to the tahini mixture and continue to fold, gently this time. Add the remaining third and fold until *just combined*. Streaks of white are okay.

Transfer the mousse to a large serving bowl and chill until set, about 5 hours. Serve the mousse with silan, pistachios, chocolate sprinkles, chocolate-covered quinoa (if using) and flaky sea salt and allow your guests to build their own mousses.

MERINGUES

TURMERIC/SESAME

Makes 12 cookies

I literally have nothing to say here about meringues. I hope you understand. They're just easy and real delicious crushed up with whipped cream . . . and fruit, I guess (a.k.a. Eton Mess). They're always overlooked, but they make a beautiful dessert.

I flavored these with a bit of turmeric and vanilla bean and topped them with black sesame seeds, but the possibilities are endless. They're exceptionally beautiful, too. I make mine rustic because I don't have the patience to clean up piping bags and tips. These irregular shapes are perfect just the way they are. You don't have to add any food coloring. I just wanted them to look more special than your boring white ones.

THE THINGS

3.3 oz (95 g) egg whites (from about 3 large eggs)

¾ cup (160 g) sugar

½ tsp cream of tartar

2 tsp (10 g) vanilla bean paste

¾ tsp ground turmeric

Pinch of kosher salt

Yellow food coloring, optional

Black sesame seeds

THE WAY

Preheat the oven to 225°F (107°C) with a rack in the middle position. Line a baking sheet with parchment paper.

In the bowl of an electric mixer fitted with a whisk attachment, whisk the egg whites on medium speed until they begin to froth, about 2 minutes. Slowly stream in the sugar while the mixer is running. Add the cream of tartar. Increase the mixer to medium-high and continue to whisk until firm peaks form, 4 to 5 minutes. Add the vanilla bean paste, turmeric, salt and enough food coloring, if using, to achieve a bright yellow color. Keep whisking until stiff peaks form.

Scoop out ¼-cup (60-ml)-size mounds onto the prepared baking sheet. I do this with a large spoon and my finger: Load the spoon with a large heap of meringue and use your index finger to swipe it off onto the baking sheet. Garnish with black sesame seeds.

Bake for 70 to 90 minutes, depending on the size of your meringues. They're set when they feel hollow and peel off the parchment easily. The outside should be crisp, and the inside, dry. Turn off the oven and allow them to cool in the oven with the door cracked open.

HOT TIPS

- Depending on the size of your meringues, they may take longer or shorter to dry out in the oven. Keep things low and slow and use your judgment when it comes to readiness.

- Serve with whipped cream (page 146) and blackberries.

- Stored in a container, these can last up to 3 days.

ICEBOX CAKE

BISCOFF/EARL GREY
CREAM

*Makes one 9-inch (23-cm)
square cake*

Israelis make a version of an icebox cake using tea biscuits and instant vanilla pudding. It's fine. Nostalgic for me, but flavor-wise it's just fine. It was one of those dishes that embarrassed me when my mom would pull it out. If you are an immigrant to the United States, you'll understand what I mean. It's a real "mouse kaka" moment from *My Big Fat Greek Wedding*.

Icebox cake is actually my favorite if it's done right. The cookie-to-cream ratio is important. Too much cream and your mouth just feels slimy and coated in fat. Too much cookie and it doesn't absorb enough moisture to get to that perfectly softened stage. Don't mess with the ratios. Definitely mess with the flavors. I've used Biscoff cookies with Earl Grey cream because it reminds me of having cookies and tea in London (I've never done that). This is a no-bake situation; a make-ahead dessert. It takes a little bit of time, but most of it is inactive.

THE THINGS

2 cups (475 ml) heavy cream

½ cup + 1 tsp (105 g) sugar

3 Earl Grey tea bags

8 oz (225 g) mascarpone cheese

Pinch of salt

2 (8.8-oz [250-g]) packages Lotus Biscoff cookies

Crumbled cookies, for garnish

THE WAY

In a heavy-bottomed pot, heat the cream and sugar over medium-high heat until the cream just begins to boil. Pour into a heatproof bowl and add the tea bags. Steep for 10 minutes. Remove the tea bags, squeezing as much cream out of them as possible. Refrigerate until the cream is cold, about 2½ hours.

In a large bowl, using an electric mixer, beat the cold cream, mascarpone and salt until medium peaks form.

Line a 9-inch (23-cm) square baking pan with parchment, leaving 2 inches (5 cm) of overhang on two opposite sides for easy lifting. Line the bottom with a single layer of cookies. Spread one-third of the whipped cream evenly over the cookie layer. Repeat 2 more times. You should have 3 layers of cookies and cream, with cream as the top layer. Cover tightly with plastic wrap and refrigerate overnight, for at least 12 hours and up to 48 hours.

Run a knife along the edges of the pan and lift out the cake. Garnish with crumbled cookies and serve cold.

HOT TIPS

- My tea bags opened up on me and I had to strain the cream. That's not a big deal.

- Try chocolate chip cookies and espresso cream.

- Make these like parfaits, in individual cups with lots of crumbled cookies for the layers.

ROASTED PEARS

HASSELBACK/SILAN/
STILTON/WALNUTS

Makes 6 servings

How do you feel about cheese with dessert? I'm a fan. And if you're still on the fence, this is a good "intro to cheese with sweets" recipe. The stars here are roasted Hasselback pears and Stilton. Stilton is one of the strongest blue cheeses I've tasted. It pairs incredibly well with pears. A little goes a long way here with the cheese.

Instead of just poaching a pear in wine, you can Hasselback a pear just as you would a potato or a halved butternut squash. It's a simple technique that makes for a more festive dish. The flavor combination in this is not something new; in fact, it's very classic (except for the silan). The simple technique here is what makes this dish different and a hell of a lot more exciting.

THE THINGS

3 Bartlett or Bosc pears

3 tbsp (42 g) unsalted butter, melted

¼ cup (85 g) silan (date syrup), plus more for drizzling

Flaky sea salt

Vanilla bean gelato

Stilton blue cheese, crumbled

Chopped walnuts

THE WAY

Preheat the oven to 375°F (190°C) with the rack in the middle position. Line a rimmed baking sheet with parchment.

Slice the pears in half through the stem and scoop out the seeds and stem with a spoon or melon baller. Place the pears, cut side down, on a cutting board. With a sharp knife, make parallel crosswise slices, about ⅛ inch (3 mm) thick, or thinner if you can, in each pear half. Take care not to cut the entire way through (see tip).

In a small bowl, combine the melted butter and silan to create a glaze.

Arrange the pears, cut side down, on the prepared baking sheet, brush generously with the silan glaze and season with a bit of flaky sea salt. Roast, glazing every 10 minutes, until the pears are cooked through and soft, 30 to 35 minutes.

Serve on top of vanilla bean gelato with crumbled Stilton, walnuts and a drizzle of silan.

HOT TIPS

- Use honey if you don't have silan on hand.

- If you're nervous about cutting through when you're cutting the pears, place a skewer on either side of the pear and cut perpendicular to the skewers. This will stop your knife from cutting down to the board.

DESSERT SALAMI

DARK CHOCOLATE/
PRETZELS/DRIED
CHERRIES

Makes 12 servings

Let's hear it again for no-bake desserts! Okay, this one is pretty cool. There is no meat in this salami. Rolled into a log and dusted with powdered sugar, it has the appearance of something you'd put on a charcuterie board with that thin layer of white mold that grows on cured meats. I saw it in a fancy chocolate shop where you can't spend less than eight dollars on a single truffle and then I saw it in Little Portugal/Little Italy in Toronto. *That's it.* I'm not sure why this hasn't become a thing yet. Maybe it has and I've just been living under a rock.

This recipe is endlessly customizable with the crunchy stuff you can add. You can change out the Lotus cookies for Oreos. You can switch out the salted pretzels for Cinnamon Toast Crunch cereal. You can leave out the dried cranberries because no one likes them, except me. Just be sure to have enough crunchy stuff and you'll be golden . . . Golden Grahams would be so good here, too, in place of the Teddy Grahams. Use what you have on hand!

THE THINGS

8 oz (225 g) good-quality dark chocolate

½ cup (120 ml) sweetened condensed milk

3½ tbsp (49 g) unsalted butter

Small pinch of kosher salt

10 Lotus Biscoff cookies, crushed, leaving lots of big pieces

½ cup (50 g) small salted pretzels, crushed, leaving lots of big pieces

⅓ cup (25 g) Honey Teddy Grahams

¼ cup (30 g) dried tart cherries

¼ cup (31 g) pistachios

¼ tsp fine espresso powder (optional)

Powdered sugar, for dusting

THE WAY

In a heatproof bowl set over a pot of lightly simmering water (or in a double broiler), melt together the chocolate, sweetened condensed milk and butter, stirring often to be sure the chocolate is melting evenly. Remove the bowl from the heat, season with a pinch of salt and mix. Add the Biscoff cookies, pretzels, Teddy Grahams, cherries, pistachios and espresso powder (if using). Mix until combined.

Immediately transfer the mixture to a long piece of plastic wrap and form into a log 2½ to 3 inches (6.5 to 7.5 cm) in diameter. Wrap very tightly in another layer of plastic wrap and chill in the fridge until hardened through, 4 to 5 hours.

Dust a rimmed baking sheet with a layer of powdered sugar. Unwrap the salami and roll it in the sugar. Shake off any excess. Roll in parchment paper and keep chilled until ready to serve.

BLONDIE #2

WHITE CHOCOLATE/ COCONUT

Makes one 9-inch (23-cm) square pan

This is a recipe from my beloved Moo Milk Bar, a bakery I built from the ground up in a little space in Toronto. It was a children's clothing store that I converted into a kitchen to sell cookies and flavored milks from. We moved to Atlanta after the first year of operation and struggled to keep it alive. It survived for another two full years before we made the hardest decision ever: to close our doors. I still get people messaging me about the recipes and asking to reopen. I'm putting it in writing here: I will reopen when the time in my life is right. When I can put all of myself into it and know that our family is settled.

This was one of our more special bar cookies that we sold. It would go just as fast as the fudgy brownies did. People would come in asking for it in hushed voices, which made me believe that I was a cocaine dealer. It basically is cocaine.

THE THINGS

Cooking spray

¾ cup + 1 tbsp (110 g) all-purpose flour

1⅓ cups (120 g) unsweetened desiccated or finely shredded coconut

1 cup + 2 tbsp (225 g) granulated sugar

½ cup (110 g) light brown sugar

1 tsp kosher salt

10 tbsp (140 g) unsalted butter

7 oz (190 g) good-quality white chocolate

3 large eggs

1½ tsp (8 g) vanilla bean paste

Powdered sugar, for dusting

THE WAY

Preheat the oven to 325°F (170°C). Grease a 9-inch (23-cm; 8-inch [20.5-cm] is fine, too) square baking pan with cooking spray and line with parchment, leaving at least a 2-inch (5-cm) overhang on two opposite sides for easy removal.

In a large bowl, combine the flour, coconut, granulated sugar, brown sugar and salt.

In a separate microwave-safe bowl, microwave the butter and chocolate in 30-second intervals, mixing in between each time, until melted and combined. Whisk in the eggs and vanilla bean paste until just combined. Add to the dry ingredients and mix until just combined.

Transfer to the prepared baking pan. Bake, in the middle of the oven, for 24 to 28 minutes, or until the edges are golden brown and the middle is just beginning to set. Remove from the oven and allow to cool to room temperature, then refrigerate for at least 3 hours before cutting. Dust with powdered sugar.

HOT TIPS

- Add chocolate chips for a coconut macaroon–type situation.

- Crumble this bar to put on ice cream.

- The batter can be used as a coconut pie filling in a buttery crust.

PANTRY
SPICE
BLENDS

SHAWARMA SPICE MIX

Makes about ½ cup (53 g)

This is my go-to basic spice mix. It's classically used to spice layers of chicken thighs and lamb fat that slowly roast on a vertical rotating spit. It's like the Middle Eastern version of Greek gyro. It's good on everything from chicken breast to vegetables to rice. I always keep this in my pantry.

3 tbsp (21 g) ground cumin

2 tbsp (14 g) ground turmeric

1 tbsp (6 g) ground coriander

1 tbsp (7 g) sweet paprika

1 tsp granulated garlic powder

½ tsp hot paprika

¼ tsp ground cloves

¼ tsp ground cinnamon

Combine all of the ingredients and store in an airtight container for up to 6 months.

BAHARAT MIX

Makes about ¼ cup (30 g)

Baharat is the Arabic word for "spices." You'll find different recipes for it depending on who is making it. Every family and shop has its own ratios. Excellent on steak.

2 tbsp (14 g) paprika

1 tbsp (7 g) ground cumin

1½ tsp (3 g) ground coriander

1 tsp freshly ground black pepper

¾ tsp ground cardamom

¾ tsp ground cinnamon

Pinch of ground nutmeg

Pinch of ground allspice

Combine all of the ingredients and store in an airtight container for up to 6 months.

THANK YOUS

This book would not have been possible without the help of my family. They've been incredibly supportive. From taking care of Zoe, to helping me create recipes in person and over the phone, to tasting something and telling me, "Nope." I love you with all my heart. Thank you to my mom, dad, savta, Yoni, Dandie, my close friends and, especially, to my husband, who are my constant support.

Thank you to my Page Street Publishing team! To Marissa, Will, Meg and anyone else who worked on making this book happen, thank you for believing in me and giving me the opportunity to write a second cookbook, which is beyond everything I ever dreamed of doing. Thank you to Marissa who told me to keep on writing and it will come when I felt that I was lost at some point. You were right!

Thank you to the readers of I Will Not Eat Oysters for helping me recipe test and brainstorm! I know the vegetarian poke bowl didn't make it into this book, but it was an awesome discussion with everyone.

Thank you to Zoe for making me a mother; something I never thought I would be so proud of. Life is exceptionally harder but also a million times better with you. Thank you for eating what I make for you and also for throwing it on the floor. Thank you for making me a better cook.

ABOUT THE AUTHOR

Danielle Oron is a recipe developer, food blogger and writer, restaurant consultant, food photographer and stylist living in Atlanta. A former chef and owner of Moo Milk Bar in Toronto, she was classically trained at the French Culinary Institute. Her Israeli and Moroccan background comes through in her cooking. She's been published in places like *The New York Times*, Yahoo Foods and Food Network, and her photography has been featured in *Bon Appétit* and *Food & Wine*. Her recipe blog, I Will Not Eat Oysters, is where she spends most of her time since becoming a mother. This is her second book with Page Street Publishing.

INDEX

P

Q

R

S